Beyond Religion Three

Some excerpts from 5 STAR reviews on Amazon and Smashwords
BEYOND RELIGION III

Brilliance at its Best! If you want something that will really give you depth and character, as well just get your brain going, pick any of Stan's work and you will not be disappointed!

Mary Leckie (Amazon.com)

… a commentary that is much needed. …brave in his writings, challenging the outdated practices and beliefs, to uncover a pureness of spirituality. With an honest approach and a humorous direct delivery this book will keep you turning the pages and eager to experience more. …an excellent read for anyone looking to broaden their horizons and examine the world around them with an unbiased mind.

Suzanne Richards (Amazon.com)

…a very deep, introspective read. This book is an excellent addition to the bookshelf of any religious scholar, philosopher, or other deep thinkers.

Jeff B (Amazon.com)

Mr. Kapuscinski's enormous base of religious, scientific, and mythological knowledge has made this trilogy a truly enlightening read. And the author's wit and humor make the text constantly enjoyable.

Ronald Piecuch

… From Adam, Eve and the famous apple to a conversation with God; love, duality and so much more there is no shortage of topics to immerse yourself in. I highly recommend it!

Amy Taylor (Smashwords.com)

…Not only is there a wealth of knowledge to occupy a healthy mind, but of course there is Law (Kapuscinski) himself who is able to bring you such powerful ideas with such eloquence and wit. …This has been a brilliant read that will take its rightful place at the top with all the books that have had a profound effect on my life.

Sid Freeman (Smashwords.com)

Other books by Stanislaw Kapuscinski

DICTIONARY OF BIBLICAL SYMBOLISM
KEY TO IMMORTALITY
DELUSIONS—Pragmatic Realism
VISULIZATION—Creating your own Universe
BEYOND RELIGION Volumes I
BEYOND RELIGION Volumes II
BEYOND RELIGION Volumes III
[Three Collections of Essays on Perception of Reality]

Fiction by Stan I.S. Law
(aka **Stanislaw Kapuscinski**)

Novels

WALL—Love, Sex, and Immortality [Aquarius Trilogy Book One]
PLUTO EFFECT [Aquarius Trilogy Book Two]
OLYMPUS—Of Gods and Men [Aquarius Trilogy Book Three]
YESHUA—Personal Memoir of the Missing Years of Jesus
PETER AND PAUL—Intuitive Sequel to Yeshûa
MARVIN CLARK—In Search of Freedom
GIFT OF GAMMAN
ENIGMA OF THE SECOND COMING
ONE JUST MAN [Winston Trilogy Book One]
ELOHIM [Winston Trilogy Book Two]
WINSTON'S KINGDOM [Winston Trilogy Book Three]
THE PRINCESS
GATE—Things my Mother told Me
ALEC [Alexander Trilogy Book One]
ALEXANDER [Alexander Trilogy Book Two]
SACHA—THE WAY BACK [Alexander Trilogy Book Three]
THE AVATAR SYNDROME [Prequel to the Headless World]
HEADLESS WORLD [Sequel to the Avatar Syndrome]
NOW—BEING AND BECOMING

Short stories

THE JEWEL AND OTHER SHORT STORIES
Sci-Fi Series 1
Sci-Fi Series 2
Cats & Dogs Series

BEYOND RELIGION III

An Inquiry into the Nature of Being
A Personal View

Stanisław Kapuściński
[aka Stan I.S. Law]

COLLECTED ESSAYS
VOLUME III

INHOUSEPRESS, MONTREAL, CANADA

Copyright © Stanislaw Kapuscinski 2001, eBooks 2010, 2014
http://stanlaw.ca
Paperback Edition 2015
All rights reserved. No part of this publication may be reproduced, stored in a retrieval system or transmitted in any form or by any means electronic, mechanical, photocopying, recording or otherwise, without the prior written permission of the publisher.

Published by
INHOUSEPRESS

INHOUSEPRESS
http://inhousepress.ca

Design and layout
Bozena Happach

ISBN 978-0-9731184-2-1

Paperback Edition 2015
INHOUSEPRESS

For my friend

Jan Jezewski

With gratitude for planting the Seed

*"Nothing exists except a-toms and empty space:
Everything else is opinion."*

Democritus of Abdera
c.460 – c.370 B.C.

CONTENTS
List of Essays

FOREWORD		11
INTRODUCTION		13

1.	XENOPHOBIA	On our genetic image and likeness	17
2.	APPLES	On fruit from several orchards	21
3.	LOVE	Why we should love our neighbour	23
4.	BEING THERE	More on being and becoming	31
5.	AN APOLOGY	On human depravation	35
6.	FATIMA	On prophesy	39
7.	ONE ON ONE	More on prophesy	45
8.	ARMAGEDDON	On making money	49
9.	THE ERRANT SUPERMAN	On assigning blame	55
10.	BLOOD BATH	On wholesale slaughter	59
11.	ETERNITY	On going to heaven	63
12.	VISUAL PERCEPTION	On the futility of reliance on our senses	66
13.	EUTHANASIA	On suffering and being human	71
14.	PROBABILITY	On quantum and other theories	75
15.	WHY THE FALL	On the reality of Eden	79
16.	BE YE PERFECT	More on duality	85
17.	THE CHICKEN & THE EGG	On the birth of the universe	89
18.	THE CHURCH	The legacy of the Roman Church	95
19.	MIRROR OF A LESSER GOD	On the advantages of marriage	99
20.	ETERNAL DAMNATION	On divine wisdom	103
21.	ECUMENISM	On faith and religion	107
22.	CONSCIOUSNESS	On human nature	113
23.	TRUTH	On the nature of God and man	117
24.	FREE WILL	Or the law of Non-interference	121
25.	SERVICE	On masters and minions	125
26.	THE MASTER	On High Self and the nature of becoming	129

List of Essays (continued)

27.	SACRIFICES	On what we must sacrifice	133
28.	HELLO?	A conversation with God	139
29.	HE GOD PARTICLE	On phenomenalists and noumenalists	143
30.	HEAVEN AND HELL	On devotional and contemplative methods	147
31.	SOUL OF A MACHINE	On Universal Soul	151
32.	SKIMMING THE SURFACE	On Pol Pot, science and karma	154
33.	THE GREEN EYED MONSTER	On envy and its insidious ways	159
34.	RUNN'N, JUMP'N AND STANDING STILL	On suburbs and teenagers	165
35.	WHO AM I?	On the search for Self	169
36.	VIRGINS	On virgins and mothers of yesteryear	173
37.	WHAT IF...	On different possibilities...	177
38.	CHILDREN	On the need for weaning	180
39.	IMMORTALITY	On liabilities and consequences	185
40.	THE FUTURE	On seeing with spiritual eyes	189
41.	MASTERS AND MINIONS	On the mastery of being	193
42.	RECUMBENT EVOLUTION	On being human	197
43.	ALL PLEASURE	On different images of divinity	201
44.	OXYMORONS AND MISNOMERS	On proper use of words	205
45.	COWORKERS	On our responsibilities	209
46.	WEALTH	On how to procure riches	213
47.	APRON STRINGS	On the future of genetics	219
48.	PERCENTAGES	On individuality	223
49.	TO KILL OR NOT TO KILL	On killing in the past and in the present	227
50.	MANIPULATORS	On the search for freedom	231
51.	TRINITY	On various entanglements in numbers	235
52.	BEYOND RELIGION III	On an impersonal Trinity	241
	POSTSCRIPT		254

All essays carry the date of original writing. Some have been somewhat updated as a result of further reading, watching and listening. The dates are given as year, month and day. Thus XENOPHOBIA had been written on 000221, i.e. on February 21, 2000

FOREWORD

It seems to me that there is but one dominant purpose to the study of reality. It is exemplified succinctly in the American constitution: The Pursuit of Happiness. We, Homo sapiens, are a very young species. Our grasp of the workings of the universe is less than elementary. One generation ago we considered an atom to be the smallest, indestructible building-block of reality. Today we dare not insist that quarks, regardless of color or flavor, qualify as the ultimate Democritus' a-toms. As the dominant species, we are still pretty ignorant. Not only in the fields of apparent esotericism but even in the areas of pure physics, all too often, the best we can do is to offer an opinion. But we mustn't worry, as Carl Sagan put it: "There is no reason to think that the evolutionary process has stopped."

There is still hope.

We abide on a minor planet orbiting an inferior sun, whose light would be invisible to a naked eye to anyone a few dozen light-years away. We have absolutely no reason to believe that we have earned any distinction among the intergalactic species. And within a galaxy consisting of billions of stars, among billions of galaxies, universe continues to expand at an absurd velocity. And then there are virtual universes, winking in and out of existence, even as virtual particles of which they are eventually formed.

In all this unimaginable grandeur, we, you and I, are put together over many millions of years from elements formed in the hearts of other, long dead stars. While most of our bodies consist of hydrogen, a star had to die to give us a few ounces of more complex atoms without which we could not survive. And thus, we and the universe are incontrovertibly interconnected. When I say We are One, we really are.

We really are.

What of the life force which motivates us to action, to thought, to higher aspirations? What of motivation towards the arts, the music, painting, sculpture, poetry? These are not the results of the ashes of the long dead stars. These are galvanized by a living force, living now, today, some say—immortal. This Force with the attributes inherent to It, particularly the attributes of infinite Knowledge and Love—I call God. All in all, driving us forward towards Its creation, towards Its countless stars, galaxies, universes, towards beauty and happiness. In the beginning there was God. The Creative Life Force. And the concomitant of this Force is Consciousness. All else comes forth from this single, omnipresent Consciousness. And there is nothing else. Visible or invisible. Manifested or virtual.

All is One. It is the attribute of this Consciousness that constitutes our reality. It is into this reality that I dive, headlong, all else being puny, transient, replaceable.

I invite you on a journey into the unknown. I hope you'll come along.

***

Education is what remains after one has forgotten everything he learned in school.

Albert Einstein

INTRODUCTION

Anyone searching these pages for quick, glib, answers will be disappointed. I would rather my readers treated my essays as a menu of exotic dishes, perhaps a silver tray of *hors-d'oeuvres*, which they might taste, relish, ponder upon their esoteric ingredients, and if still tempted—swallow.

Whatever subject is discussed in these pages, it is always, *per force*, colored by my attitude towards reality as I see it. A friend once told me that I do not provide straight answers to the multitude of questions raised. I don't, according to him, even provide sufficient meat to engage in a profound discussion.

That's quite true. What I offer is a view of reality that is *not* espoused by the vast majority of people I've ever met. The intend of my essays is not to impose my views on others, but to inspire the reader to form his or hers own viewpoint which will not be limited by the evidence of their senses or conditioning.

We all see reality differently.

Beauty to some is dire boredom or indifference to others. We hear differently. Hard-rock is reputed to be music to some ears, jarring cacophony to others. A gentle touch is but a sign of weakness to those hankering for power. Tastes in food differ the world over. And so on. And what seems even worse (or better?) is that all tastes, all opinions derived from the evidence of our senses appear to be transient, ephemeral. We live, hopefully we grow, we mature. We become more discriminating. We evolve. Physically, mentally, perhaps even at the spiritual levels. This last motley is usually dismissed as superstition, unrealistic, impractical—unreliable. Yet, by the Sherlock Holmes' well-known process of exclusion, the spiritual reality seems the only one that is permanent, unchanging, and reliable.

Whoever read my essays collected in Volumes I and II, must have a good idea what direction I have chosen in my study of reality. I searched, and continue searching, not just for the Truth *per se*, but into the manner in which modern man/woman can incorporate this Truth in his/her everyday life. After some twenty-five years of study, I came to the conclusion that once we find the key, which unlocks the knowledge seated deeply in our unconscious, our viewpoint changes dramatically. I have already demonstrated, however briefly, the futility of reliance on our senses. Unfortunately, for as long as we limit ourselves to the constrains of our intellect, we remain in dualistic reality. It is still a reality of contrasts, contradictions, and apparent mysteries so dear to most if not all world religions. As long as we wish to perform miracles, to act as an intermediary between the Potential and the Consequence, we espouse a dualistic, transient, ephemeral mode. We accept a reality that is not as good as it could be. On the other hand, the Perfection, referred to by some people as God, does *not* appear to be omnipresent. Unless we revise our definition of Perfection. If God were as defined by religions, there would be no need for miracles. God, who is perfect and omnipresent, precludes any necessity for improvement.

And yet...?

Hence the essays.

In the meantime, it seems that only spiritual reality offers escape from duality. It is passive, static, eternal, undisturbed, inexplicable bliss. If you join me on my journey, our search will not lead us to stop performing miracles, but to perform them only for those who still have need of them. For those who have not yet achieved liberation from the dualistic mode of being. We all perform and witness miracles daily. The trick is to see them with non-physical senses. To witness them as eternal observers and then to realize that we and the Observer are one.

***

*How do you know but every bird
that wings the airy way,
Is an enormous world of delight,
Closed to your senses five?*

William Blake
(1757—1827)

1

XENOPHOBIA

And God created man unto his image and likeness.
We continue to do so. If our own creations veer from our likeness, we call them retarded, stupid, maladjusted, or just ungrateful brats who do not appreciate all that we have done for them. Just look around. The streets are full of homeless kids with pierced ears, noses, eyebrows and probably brains. They are the vagabonds, looking for love in a beer-bottle, a needle, a reefer, or any other quick fix. We, the parents, have created their environment. We, the parents, repudiate any responsibility for their actions. Just as they do—the squeegee kids.
They are different. They do not conform.
They are not in our image and likeness.

If Einstein had spawned you or me, the illustrious entourage of egg-heads would probably regard our actions and mental ability as dismal. Retarded. I have a friend who's child is much less retarded in relations to him than we are in relation to Einstein, yet the doleful father suffers because he regards his progeny as not 'normal'. Little does he know that 'normal' means average, uninteresting, dull, one of the masses. By wanting your child to be normal you sentence him/her to mediocrity.

Xenophobia—the fear of the different, of that which is strange to us.
Ultimately, the fear of the unknown.

Being different from us is not limited to the extraterrestrials landing their bits of crockery in our backyards. Xenophobia is alive and well in the hearts of frustrated fathers and mothers whose children dare to be, to have been born, different. No doubt we think ourselves so perfect that any deviation from our mould, our paradigm, we regard with alarm, disdain, often disgust.

Strangely enough, only deviations, or what the scientists call mutations, have assured our evolution. And what is more, the basis for our animosity towards that which is different has a purely genetic background. For our species to survive, our genes must have spurned all other genes for millions of years. If we limit ourselves to such a mindset, then we, guided by our genes, will continue to do so. If we can rise above such a primitive level then we can extend what Carl Sagan calls "the identification horizon" not only to other species but also to the whole world.[1]

Why can't everyone be like us? We ask. Aren't *we* good enough?

Certainly not if we are xenophobic. For whatever reason.

In my recent book VISUALIZATION[2], I have listed a number of unlikely candidates for being recognized as retarded, together with their apparent deficiencies: "Albert Einstein and the renown author Virginia Wolf were unable to speak until they were three years old. As a child, the sculptor Auguste Rodin was so inept at reading and math that his parents and teachers discouraged him even from his passion for art. The multimillionaires of the entertainment industry, Tom Cruise, Cher, Whoopi Goldberg and Henry Winkler are dyslexic (unable to grasp the meaning of that which is read). So had been Leonardo da Vinci and Winston Churchill. Louis Pasteur had problems with math while George Washington couldn't spell." I can only repeat that the problems these people faced were theirs to overcome. And they have been.

The first paintings of the impressionists had been regarded by the connoisseurs as 'retarded', and bought for pittance by the backward dilettanti from Russia. The Russian ignoramuses are now millionaires, western connoisseurs—dead and forgotten. The rest is history. Or evolution. But there is also devolution. The physical universe suffers from a deadly disease called entropy. We can succumb to it and cooperate with the elimination of that which is different, or we can rise above it and rejoice in our abundant diversity.

Different is not bad, certainly not abnormal, but, all too often, super-normal. The absence of the average-gene in a son or a daughter is often compensated by a unique, extraordinary talent. It may be a capacity to paint or sculpt in a manner heretofore unknown. It may be a new resonance in musical structures, new approach to other art-forms; it may be an ability to love, to spread cheer and smile in areas where 'normal' people would be hard-pressed to find a ray of hope. It may take a long while to discover their unique gift. But the moral is simple. Do not judge, and particularly pre-judge. He who is different from us is not worse. He or she might well be better. Perhaps a mutant. A genius? Only time will tell.

I know of a world chess champion that could not tie his shoelaces.

Was he sub-normal?

To my knowledge no child prodigy ever survived our educational system. Oscar Wild said that he never allowed his schooling to interfere with his education.

Yet, we all remain xenophobic. To a degree.

The clever among us fear abject stupidity, the rich fear the poor, the poor—the rich. God forbid our daughter deemed to marry someone of a different skin hue. Perversely, the opposites invariably attract each other, simply because the dualistic reality demands it of the opposites. An electron is attracted to a proton—as mentioned before, the rest is history.

We are not equipped to judge our children. We can only attempt to help them as best we can. What if they cannot cope in school? Just how many geniuses have our educational systems produced? On the other hand, how many successful graduates have swollen the ranks of crooks, murderers, dishonest politicians, greedy lawyers or perverts masquerading under some disguise? The children who are 'different' will never be any of these. They are and will remain the unique, precious gifts reaching out from the divine into our midst.

It is we who are retarded by wanting to bring all to a common denominator.

Neither we nor our children are limited to our bodies, even minds. We are spiritual entities experimenting with different modes of being. The sooner we accept this truth the sooner we shall free ourselves from our genetic psychosis, from xenophobia. And we shall allow our children to develop their own image and likeness. To be themselves.

And then, within the abundant ocean of mediocrity, let us hope, none of them shall ever become normal.

***

000221

FOOTNOTES

(1). Sagan, Carl THE COSMIC CONNECTION [Dell publ. Co., Inc.. New York 1973]

(2). Kapuscinski, Stanislaw VISUALIZATION / CREATING YOUR OWN UNIVERSE. [Inhousepress, Montreal 2000, Amazon Kindle 2010, Paperback 2015]

2

APPLES

When offering **Adam an apple,** Eve pulled a fast one. Who could resist Eve—whatever she had to offer? She was the only game in town. I'm sure she polished the pome, gingerly, on her silky skin, till it shone with the fire of gold. For a man whose fridge was still out of order, a tempting snack indeed. Nevertheless, we are told, the price of a single bite was the expulsion from Eden. One can but wonder what else Eve had to offer. A rotten trick, you might say, or, if we choose to interpret the parable literally (as so very many still do), perhaps a rotten apple?

Apples always appear to have brought problems to mankind. The Greek goddess Eris, annoyed at not having been invited to a wedding, threw—not a tantrum, but—an apple. It was a gorgeous, golden apple, marked "for the most beautiful". Immediately Hera, Athena and Aphrodite claimed the fruit, each for herself. You know women... Strife followed, all because of an apple. Prince Paris, the son of Priam the king of Troy, managed to get hold of this very same apple and, for reasons of his own, offered it to the "most beautiful" Aphrodite. In gratitude for the recognition (not to mention flattery), the goddess of beauty helped Paris to kidnap Helen, thus plunging the known world into the long lasting Trojan War. Have you noticed how much trouble a single apple can make? Of course the involvement of a beautiful woman doesn't hurt any either. The Greeks knew that. They named the fruit the *apple of discord*, Eris—the goddess of discord.

After all this apple-trouble one can but wonder why the goddess Aphrodite is not mythologically connected to the tomato. Were not tomatoes originally known as apples of love, or love-apples?

I really like tomatoes...

Many years ago a great man said that we could recognize the quality of the tree by it's fruit, rather like being able to tell the quality of an apple tree by the apples it produces. If the apples are bitter, rotten, devoid of quality, then any reasonable man would cut the apple tree down, to make room for another. If one didn't do so after a season or two, one certainly wouldn't postpone the pruning, let alone outright cutting down, for thousands of years. Too risky. One bad apple tree might pollute or infect the whole orchard. Great danger lurks in procrastination of what one must or should do. Whatever it is.

Perhaps that's why we have developed systems with built-in checks and balances. There are tiers of agencies designed to assure that the tree of the government does not bear rotten apples—at least, not... for too long. Not for long enough to infect the orchard itself. Only dictatorships, be they outright or oligarchic, defy this wisdom. And they fall. As Napoleon, Mussolini, Hitler, Stalin, as Communism have fallen. Evil dictators and evil empires. Rotten apples. Trees tainted with greed, with the excesses of power, with megalomania.

And hence the paradox.

There is an organization that ascended to power riding the crest of the orchard. It is also the sole organization that acts in total defiance of the teaching on which it bases its authority. After two millennia of rotten, bitter, deceitful apples, of apples which caused more discord that Eris could ever do, the presiding Pontifex Maximus, the boss of bosses, rose in his splendiferous attire and proclaimed that although the apples may be rotten-to-the-core, the apple-tree itself is perfect. He said 'sorry' about the apples, but... the tree is good. In fact, perfect. The boss-of-bosses said so with a straight face, as though believing that the words spewing from of his mouth weren't in total denial of him who said, "by their fruits ye shall know them." Admittedly, there have also been one or two, perhaps even a few, apples that bore evidence of quality. But they really were but few and far between. In fact it would be all too easy to find many orchards which bore vastly superior fruit to the one the boss-of-bosses is so adamant in defending.

Why? Could it be lust for power? If the present Infallible One is any example then the answer must be—yes. The lust for power so implacable, so grim, so relentless, that the stooping, all-but-collapsing old man, hardly able to mumble almost inaudible words, let alone stand up straight or walk, refuses to let go. And yet what power? Isn't the Kingdom he swore to protect not of this world? And if such is the case, does this real Kingdom need protection? Why, then, such single-minded determination to dominate all other orchards here-and-now? Why create conditions wherein rotten apples grow in such dismal abundance? *"We forgive and we ask forgiveness,"* he said several times. No specific wrongdoings.

Not one.

Are we supposed to guess?

Could he have been talking about the late Middle Ages when his predecessors carried out the Inquisition in which the non-believers had been tortured and killed in their thousands?[1] Or perhaps the later revived Spanish version that was even more brutal?[2] Or was he asking forgiveness for the thousands of Muslims slaughtered by the Christian soldiers in a bid to reclaim the Holy Land—all under the aegis of the Holy See? Or could it be that the hatred diffused over many centuries by his *Holy* organization against the Jews finally bore fruit in the death camps of the Second World War? A rotten fruit indeed. Or was the apology directed at the official and officious degradation of women, even within his own organization? Or perhaps he was referring to the mistreatment of all the minorities as some inferior children of a lesser God?

Surely, he could not have been talking about the hundreds, perhaps thousands, of boys brutally treated by his sodomitical priesthood? Or the horror stories only recently surfacing about the abuses in the orphanages run under his infallible protection by such innocent looking nuns? Or perhaps he was thinking about the Nazi money laundered through the Vatican bank, the Church bank, the bank of the Holy, Pristine, Unscathed, eternally Innocent Church? We shall never know.

The apology: *"...cannot assume the aspect of a spectacular self-flagellation"* insisted Cardinal Roger Etchegary, president of the Vatican's 2000 Jubilee Committee. Cardinal Joseph Ratzinger, head of the Congregation for the Propagation of the Faith (which articulates church dogma) said that the Catholic theology prevents the Pontiff from apologizing for any wrongs of the Roman Catholic Church itself.

So many, so very many, rotten, bitter apples. All from a single, so fruitful a tree. It makes you indeed believe in miracles. Unless... unless you believe him who told the parable that "a good tree *cannot* bring forth evil fruit".[3]

Hence the apple of Sodom. The Dead Sea apple. It is thus described by Josephus[4], the thoroughly Romanized Jewish historian and soldier: *"...which fruit have the color as if they were fit to be eaten; but if you pluck them with your hands they dissolve into smoke and ashes."* Hence anything of promising appearance which disappoints and deceives. Perhaps we should beware of anyone, or anything, being thoroughly Romanized.

***
000314

FOOTNOTES

(1). Matthew 7:17/18. (my emphasis)
(2). Josephus, Flavius A.D. 37—A.D.95 (?)
(3). The 12th through 15th centuries.
(4). between 1500 and 1834

3

LOVE

More has been written on the subject of this four-letter-word than on any other subject. More nonsense has been garnished with this apparently inexhaustible staple than seems possible for the rampant imagination of man. Empires have been built and lost; heroes have been elevated to Olympian heights; gods have been conjured and murdered, as have thousands of their followers—all in the name of love. Love of what? Power? Beauty? Prolific riches, Faustian talents, beguiling secrets of an enticing woman?

Some say that love is the greatest power on earth. Isn't love the very antithesis of power? Perhaps it is the most irresistible force, rather than power.

What limits the efficacy of love is not its own frailty but capacity of the recipient to accept it. A deaf man cannot accept the love encapsulated in the harmonies of a musical masterpiece; a blind man cannot appreciate the ebullience of the old masters, or the shimmering light of the impressionist. Nor can we experience love if we close the floodgates through which it threatens to overwhelm us. And finally, until we realize that love is not a feeling, an emotion, but the most irresistible force binding the universes together, we shall never experience true love.

And thus we are told: *Thou shalt love the Lord thy God with all thy heart, and with all thy soul, and with all thy mind...*[1]

So many of my good friends file out, dutifully, to their many churches (almost) every Sunday, presumably looking for their God and, once there, they proceed to love Him as best they can. Yet, how can they? How can they love what to most of them is a mystery? Who is this mysterious *Lord?* Can one love a God one never experienced? Surely, one cannot love what one does not understand. When Spinoza said "to define God is to deny God", he merely refused to set limitations which such a definition might impose. He did not advocate abject ignorance of the source of Life, on the Source of All. And most of all, the Source of Love Itself. But the ignorance of my brothers and sisters doesn't stop there. My dear, honest, truly decent friends have only the vaguest idea what is this *heart* they are supposed to commit to such a task. They seem to have an even lesser idea of what is *soul*, and only a vague impression of the real function of their *mind.*

Let us try to eliminate all 'mystery' from the commandment.

You are the Lord.

You are the sole architect shaping reality from the inexhaustible abundance of the Universal Creative Spirit. You create your universe, your truth. You are the Truth. According to what you believe in—that becomes your life, your health, your joy, your wealth, your pleasure. God, the ineffable, the unimaginable, incommunicable, indescribable, inexpressible, unspeakable... will forever, as Spinoza would say, remain indefinable.[2] God the Spirit, the unchangeable, immutable Source, the Father, is That from which all draws its substance. But since, as far as you are concerned, *your* power is infinite, the Lord, the High Self, the I AM, the Living Christ, the Only Son of God is *de facto*—God. The Lord and God-the-Father are identical in 'quality', though not in 'quantity'. One cannot tell the difference between a single drop of saline water and the rest of the ocean, because *their nature is identical*. At this level of perception you were never born, you will never die. YOU ARE even as I AM. There is no outside agency, no outside interference that has the power to influence you against your will. Jehovah (the Lord) confessed to Moses that His name is I AM, and He warned that *thou shalt have none other Gods before me*.[3] The Lord is thy God. And none other. Fifteen hundred years later he who showed us the way said: I *and my father are one*. Inseparable. The same truth promulgated centuries apart.

Will people ever understand?

It is this God *within* that we are admonished to love. And love, in this elevated state, means to *become one with*. To lose the boundary where you cease and the Lord begins. To become One. Are we any closer to understanding who is this God? We must defy Spinoza once more. God is not just the fountain of life. God is LIFE Itself. To love God is to love Life. It is to love immortality. *I am the resurrection and the life*[4] Create your own list of perfections, of abundant life, of beauty, of harmony and order, of love and compassion, of unimaginable wealth, of the realization of all your indestructible dreams... *and then fall in love with them*. When you do, you will love God. You will love Love Itself. If you settle for any less, for any imperfection, any blemish, then you don't love God but some lesser deity. You will create yourself unto an image and likeness of a lesser god. Only perfection is acceptable. Be ye perfect.[5]

It is that simple.

And what of soul?

Soul spelled with a capital S, is defined above. It is the I AM. It is a mode of being. Soul is but one and It is the expression of the divine attribute of Individualization. In you and in me. In all of us. In animals and plants. In rocks and grains of sand on a distant beach. In stars and galaxies. In the vastness of space. Without end.

Soul spelled with the lower case: 'soul', represents the sum total of all that you (the individualized I AM) have accomplished, from the beginning of time, towards the realization described above. It is your subconscious. It is your feminine aspect, your anima, which defines and nurtures that which you are. And the very essence of your soul that controls your thoughts, your behavior, is your *heart*. You must learn to love Life, Perfection, not only with your conscious mind, but also with the totality of your being. The desire for and the love of Perfection in all Its Attributes must be instilled in your *heart*. This means your total subconscious must be impregnated with it. When it is, your soul will be worth saving. Every aspect of you will be preserved for eternity. You will give an individual expression to the Universality.

And what of your mind?

The *mind* is the means, the executive function. Every miracle is a miracle of the mind. Mind is the machine, the instrument, which creates reality. Whatever your mind dwells on, for any length of time, sooner of later becomes manifest in this, the material world. When you want something, you must ask, insist if you like, in the name of your High Self, by the power of your Mind. The authority is there at your disposal. It is your ultra mind. Your super-consciousness. It is your dream factory. When you learn to love God, when you learn to employ the creative force exclusively for the good of the Universal, you will have learned to *love with your mind*. You will have learned to love yourself. Your true, real Self. And since the individualized Soul is one and the same in every being, in all of creation, you will love God in your family, your neighbors, in your friends and associates. You will discover Him in all His modes of being. Throughout the universes. For ever. And since love unites, you will never, *never*, be alone.

Isn't it fun?

A church, any church, of any religion, has only two functions. First, to teach and assure every man, woman and child that God is within his or her own being. And the second is just as straightforward. Since this statement is true of every one of us, surely, we must, *per force*... love one another. What we really love is the God manifested in and through each one of us.

This is what love is all about.

It has been said that as you rise in consciousness towards the bliss of heaven, your power increases enormously. Yet, when you finally "get there", all you find is Love.

***

000315

FOOTNOTES

(1). Matthew 22:37
(2). Baruch or Benedict Spinoza (1632-77). In 1656 the Jewish group in which he was raised had excommunicated him for independence of thought.
(3). Deuteronomy 5:7
(4). John 11:25
(5). Matthew 5:48, *perfect* from Greek *teleios* also meaning *complete*.

O foolish mind,
why do you go here and there in search of Lord Vishnu,
when He is very much present in you?

Teluga poem

4

BEING THERE

Three men, from very different walks of life, inspired my today's soliloquy. Peter Sellers—the inimitable comedy actor, Joseph Campbell—whose knowledge of the world's myths surpasses all scholars I've ever read, and the genius of the century himself, Albert Einstein. All three men cast a unique view on the human condition of being, of what it is that makes us alive. All three suggest that the withdrawal of our facility to help others is contiguous to the aging process, which in many ways is equivalent to no longer being useful to our fellowman. This withdrawal, in turn, is not resultant from the onset of any physical limitations or inadequacies, but only and solely from our state of mind, our firm belief, no matter how untrue, that we no longer have anything to offer. We shall see that the attendant decrepitude is the consequence of laziness, of indolence, which is the only cause of most if not all our problems related to aging.

We do not age in our body, we age in our minds.

The first example is, of course, taken from the melancholy satirical comedy film: Being *There*. In it, the character played by Peter Sellers personifies a gardener who, having been transplanted from his habitual environment, begins to dwell, abide, in abject passivity. *Being There* becomes an indolent, supine, substitute for "Doing Anything Anywhere", to being useful. The epitome of this condition is so unnatural to the human nature that the 'gardener' is assigned superhuman traits of character, practically divine ability, which just "being there" can foster. God *is*, we are merely—becoming. The gardener *is*, therefore he is divine. He is also dead from the neck up. Hence the satire.[1]

This attitude brings me to Joseph Campbell. In one of his wonderful lectures, he affirmed that throughout history man's job was to *do*, a woman's to *be*. A man had to remain active; to do, to perform, to be engaged in producing, fighting, defending, in supplying whatever was necessary for the woman to 'be'. In my essay on *Being and Becoming*, I stress the validity of the state of 'being' as against that of 'becoming'.[2] To be is to have achieved, to have reached, to have succeeded in one's endeavor, dream, ambition. To be in a state of becoming, is to remain on the journey, to admit one's inadequacy of not having, as yet, scaled the insurmountable mountain. It is to be a transient, a pilgrim on the way. Yet is also means *to be alive*.

If we accept Campbell's dictum, a woman by being has achieved her purpose.

If we also accept the concept of death, of singularity of temporal existence, then the above would be true. Luckily, all evidence points to reincarnation, wherein man conquers new horizons only to be given a chance to consolidate his findings in his next life, in which he will inhabit the body of a woman. A woman nurtures, protects—*is* that which she achieved in her (his) previous incarnation. There are exceptions, of course. There are very passive men, very active woman. Perhaps this is what Jesus said to his disciples in the Gospel of Thomas "I'll make her male".[3] If we were to concentrate on becoming all the time, we would never really learn if our new knowledge could be put to practice. We would be so busy chasing after a rainbow that we would not notice being awash in its glorious rays. A woman can be—by being there. But she pays a price. She must be more passive. Her role of activity has often been confined to sharing her state of being, of providing a haven in the ocean of living, of providing the stable rock in turbulent waters of life. If she refuses to do so, the raging current may sweep both him and her. It is wise to think of life as continuity, of alternating between being and becoming, lest we forget what it is that we have become.

Yet there we must be careful. It is much easier to be active than passive-yet-alive. Perhaps that is why men are said to offer their efforts—women proffer themselves. To be the latter, we must not only share with others our inherent knowingness, but we must actively observe and record the consequences of this sharing. There will be little time for such digression in our next life, when we shall be busy, once again, reaching beyond the new horizons.

And this leads us directly to Albert Einstein.

He once said: *"Man like every other animal is by nature indolent. If nothing spurs him on, then he will hardly think, and will behave from habit like an automaton."* Perhaps the genius was contemplating on his own passivity. It seems that Einstein's greatest achievement took place early in his life. Later, he... coasted. Or so he thought. Frankly, I think that he became so weighed by his novel vision of the world, of cosmos, that he began the process of consolidation already in his present life. There is only so much a man can do in a single lifetime. Einstein's thoughts embraced the whole universe. A tough nut to swallow, er... follow.

But was he right? Are we indolent animals by nature?

I'm very much afraid so.

Most people remain active for as long as they must. By that I mean that man works instinctively only for as long as he supports his family. A woman does her share, until her progeny has weaned. Then, both put on weight (a sort of insurance), become more passive, more sedate. Why work when I don't have to?

We are definitely indolent by nature.

If we do not think of ourselves as being useful to someone, we slow down. Mentally, we lie down and wait to die. This, of course, makes us indolent animals, not humans. To be human is to be much more then to propagate our species. It is, ultimately, to learn two universal tenets. One, that we are all one, and two, that we are immortal. That if we become passive without sharing, than the whole humanity loses something in the process. No matter how old, we have a great deal to offer. Perhaps, the greatest challenge is to find what it is. To find it and to share that knowledge, that knowingness, with others. And this is so much more suited to a woman than a man. A man must be active. If he cannot run around, he feels inadequate. Not all man. Stephen Hawking stopped running around many years ago, yet remained active. But a woman is not limited by such constrains of character. She can continue to be, to shine, to share, and to give of herself. No matter how old, love can pour in great abundance from an experienced heart. When this happens, the years seem to peel away as if by magic.

Perhaps love has no age. Perhaps love just is.

***

000329

FOOTNOTES

(1). For those unfamiliar with my apriorism: God *is*, but His mode of being is in us, and we are in the eternal mode of becoming. We are the entities through which God experiences the condition of change. God is Life, but we are the *living*.

(2). BEYOND RELIGION, Collected Essays, Volume I. [Inhousepress, Montreal 1997]

(3). Kapuscinski, Stanislaw KEY TO IMMORTALITY, *The Gospel according to Thomas*, logion 114 (Inhousepress, Montreal 2000, Amazon Kindle 2010).

Have you heard the music that no fingers enter into?

Kabir
[A mystic poet and saint of India, 1440—1518]

5

AN APOLOGY

There are many who found shortcomings in the recent papal apology for the misdeeds of the Roman Catholics committed over the centuries. We can only hope that whoever speaks for the Protestants, the Muslim, the Jews, the Hindûs, and other religions whose palms carry Macbethian stains will offer a more complete apology for the misdeeds of their sacerdotal members.

Is it likely to happen?

Whatever the papal apology, the sins of the Catholics certainly do not stand alone. Nor are the malefactors of neither other religions nor other secular organizations. Others, many others, dipped their long arms into other people's pockets, stained them up to their elbows with other people's blood. Kings and queens, presidents and prime ministers, generals and admirals, dictators and elite members of depraved oligarchies, countless perfidious aristocrats, all, ALL are guilty as charged. Or as innocent... even as the Roman Church is innocent, according to the Holy Father. Power corrupts everyone equally. This is what power does. It always did.

Yet none of the perpetrators are likely to ever follow even in the faltering papal footsteps. None of them will ever admit to their crimes against humanity. Like the Roman Church, they will forever remain innocent. Or perhaps like

Pinochet: "guilty but insane". Perhaps they were: "Just carrying out orders". Only their hands will remain bloodied. And therefore, it is in their name, in the name of all people in power, that I apologize. *Urbi et orbi.* Even as the pope did, so that the guilty might remain innocent.

For the many humans being so profoundly subhuman, I apologize.

For the war-to-end-all-wars and didn't, and the next war that ignited the whole world—*I apologize.* For the countless millions of lives lost under the Communist and Nazi rules; for the concentration camps and for prisons; and for Siberia—*I apologize.*

For the bloodshed in the Chino-Japanese War, the Spanish Civil war; for the wars in Korea and Vietnam, and the subsequent loss of lives and limbs of adults and children alike in the insidious minefields—*I apologize.*

For the murderous civil wars in Nicaragua, Panama, El Salvador, and for the heinous abuses of power in Argentina and Chile; for the bloodthirsty rebellion of the Sandero Luminoso in Peru who murdered as many members of the "upper classes" as they did peasants in whose name they reaped their bloody harvest—*I apologize.*

For the ongoing crimes of countless drug-lords throughout North, Middle and South America, Europe and Asia, the Middle and the Far East, the world over, for poisoning the minds and bodies of our children and the exploitation of their innocence for sex traffic—*I apologize.*

For the persistent mass murders of innocent peasants of whom an estimated two million have died by execution, starvation, disease or overwork during the rule of the Maoist-inspired Khmer Rouge in Cambodia—*I apologize.*

For the senseless war between Iran and Iraq, for using children on the front lines of the battles while the generals and imams grew fatter in safety—*I apologize.*

AN APOLOGY

For tribal cleansing in Iran, Algiers, Sudan, Ethiopia, Libya, by equally vicious religious expurgations in many of the republics of befallen USSR, and for all other crimes inspired by Moslem fundamentalists, for the Christian-Moslem-Hindu genocidal strife in India, Sri Lanka, Indonesia—*I apologize*.

For the genocidal wars, murders, tortures, exploitations, abuses in South Africa, Sudan, Somalia, Sierra Leone, and still going on in Congo and Uganda, on and on and on... all over the starving Africa—*I apologize*.

For the invasion of Kuwait by Iraq and the consequent brutal Western military response, for the homicidal games played by the Protestants and Roman Catholics in Ireland, for the Chinese invasion of Tibet, for Tiananmen Square massacre, for the murderous nonsense of Falkland islands, for the bloodthirsty ethnic cleansing in the defunct Yugoslavia which reached its utter ignominy in Bosnia, Kossovo, Albania, for the laying waste of Chechnya, for all of them—*I apologize*.

...for all the wars yet to come for which no one will ever apologize— in the name of all humanity I'm sorry.
I am really sorry...

For centuries of abuse and exploitation by the greatest crime organization of all time, the British Empire, for France's and Portugal's cruelty in the subjugation of their former colonies, and for all the empires which came before them, empires which usurped riches while creating poverty—*I apologize*.

For as Mahatma Gandhi had said: Poverty *is the greatest crime*.

And thus, for all of us who eat more then we should, or need to, when others go hungry—*I apologize*.

In the name of each and ever man who ever wielded power in whatever name, *I apologize*. In the name of humanity for all who are still imperfect, I apologize because my church is not innocent. I, and my church, my orchard—the human race—we are all guilty as charged.

For all these that I've listed, and so many I haven't...
I apologize.
Surely, someone should?
Shall we all be forgiven?
Will anyone listen?
Care?

***
000331

Father, forgive them: for they know not what they do.

Luke 23:34

6

FATIMA

Dreams, visions, insights, can be the by-product of excessive intake of good wine, of hitting one's head against a wall, inordinate fatigue, or even lugubrious ennui. In other words, when our senses no longer transmit their input relating objective reality, the reality we share with other people, we slip into our private subjective world. Such dreams and visions fade into oblivion, as they should, the moment we recover from our temporary deviation from the norm. We sober up, our head stops hurting.

And then, there is the second group of revelations.

There are other dreams and visions which, given a chance, we should attempt to take much more seriously. This other kind is an attempt of our unconscious to communicate with our conscious mind which, for the most part, is held in an iron grip of our subconscious. As I have discussed in previous essays, our *sub*conscious is the sum-total of our material experience that enables our physical bodies to survive within an ever-changing physical environment.

Our *un*conscious is a very different cattle of fish.

Not only it is not concerned with our physical survival, but also it provides us with the only link with that which is indestructible, permanent, static, eternal. It is the narrow gate through which the Ocean of Infinite Possibilities attempts to communicate with our mundane awareness. Since the two states of consciousness have little in common, they have not, as yet, established a common means of communication. For the unconscious, or more precisely our unchangeable state of consciousness, the I AM, to communicate with our physical awareness *through* the unconscious, It employs symbols, allegories or images to convey Its messages. At the broadcast end of the communication these messages are holistic, *gestält* concepts, and by the time our conscious mind educes any understanding of them, they degenerate into two or three-dimensional images, what Carl Yung called *archetypes*, or merely very vague impressions. It takes a lifetime of study to learn to recognize them, to separate them from the continuous clutter of random thoughts invading our mind, to still our mind long enough to become aware of them. By the time we attempt to convey such images or impressions to other people, we are forced to translate them into linguistically structured communication, into words of a language, into a horizontally projected symbols.

Imagine describing a magnificent painting to a blind person by identifying each individual stroke the artist placed on the canvas, from the upper left corner of the painting down, in a series of horizontal lines, to the right bottom corner. Yet this is how we communicate with each other, this is what I am doing right now, in attempting to convey to you my understanding of what an inspired, holistic, gestält vision becomes when put down on a piece of paper.

And this brings us to Fatima.

Three girls, still unspoiled by the impositions of our cultural disciplines or a written language, were capable of recognizing a vision, a communication from their common unconscious. Children are much more likely to perform such feats than adults, who have learned to dismiss all inputs from their unconscious as drivel, or resulting from causes which I have listed at the start of this essay. Cardinal Joseph Ratzinger, the head of the Vatican's Congregation for the Doctrine of the Faith, is no exception. He attempted to interpret the 'vision' from a document written down by one of the children. Not only is it practically impossible to translate any 'real' vision into words, but the very words have been written down by a child not within days, weeks or even months after the experience, but by a nun, Lucia dos Santos, (now 93 years old and the only survivor of the three children who shared the vision) in 1944, fully 27 years after her experience.[1]

To worsen the case, Cardinal Ratzinger seems quite unaware of the symbolic nature of all 'inspired' visions. He must have forgotten that his avowed Master, the Christ, spoke almost exclusively in parables, in allegories, in symbolic images, to convey what his unconscious was communicating to him. Could the three children have been so much smarter? Could it be that their images must be taken as close to being mundane forecasts of physical events that were to have taken place sometime in some undefined future?

What utter balderdash!

No fundamentalist doctrine can ever do justice to the truth, which originates in our unconscious. We may forever remain ignorant, we might never fully appreciate what the children have said, but trying to interpret their vision in terms of physical events related to living, physical men, is to debase them into total nonsense.

Furthermore, no one can interpret another person's vision for a third party.[2] Not with any precision. The communication with the 'spirit' is *always* a one-on-one transaction, as it is directly related to, and dependent on, the development of the consciousness of the 'receiver'. To interject oneself between God and man is to deny the very essence of the teaching of the New Testament. God, we are told, is in heaven and heaven is within you. Any other postulate is a willful perversion of the original teaching. As for the attempting to get 'close' to what the children "might have seen", let us attempt to list a few basic steps.

Purportedly, the children saw *"a bishop dressed in white (and) we had an impression that it was the Holy Father,"* (again, as purportedly written by a nun 27 years after the event). Later on, in this written statement, the children saw (we have the nun's word for it), the Pope[3] *"passing through a big city half in ruins and half trembling with halting step, afflicted with pain and sorrow (and) he prayed for the souls of corpses he met on his way."* When the Pope reached the top of a mountain and was praying at the foot of a cross, *"he was killed by a group of soldiers who fired bullets and arrows at him"* even as he and other bishops, priest and nuns and other people *"died one after the other."* Angels then *"gathered up the blood of the martyrs and with it sprinkled the souls that were making their way to God."*

A tragic vision indeed.

The Vatican waited till recently to release the text of this apocalypse. Could it be that only now the scholars could concoct a story that the faithful might swallow? Apparently (according to Vatican sources) the 'prophetic' events described in vision already took place; only the group of soldiers armed with the bullets and arrows have been reduced to a single Turkish gunman Mahmed Ali Agca, who in 1981 shot and nearly killed the Pope. Only... the Pope recovered (perhaps resurrected?) and, to top it all, the Pope the children saw was none other than our very own John Paul II! As for other bishops, priest and other people... well, they didn't actually die in the attempt on the Holy Father's life. In fact no one was injured at all. Furthermore, there was hardly any blood, so the angels had very little to gather, let alone sprinkle on souls...

Then the Ratzinger doctrine expands to deal with communism, political systems in Eastern Europe, all derived by some miraculous interpolation from the three little children.

And this is the story Cardinal Ratzinger, the guardian of the Doctrine of the Faith, is sticking to. Furthermore, before the Vatican decided to reveal the third part of the Fatima 'secret' to the world at large, the papal envoys visited Sister Lucia, who reportedly immediately agreed with the Pope's own interpretation of the vision conveyed to her, and apparently with equal alacrity confirmed that the Pope was indeed *the* Pope, J-P II. It is interesting to note that when the children received their vision, John Paul, or even Karol Wojtyła, hadn't been born yet. Nevertheless, the mystery, the secret so jealously guarded by the Vatican since 1944 is finally ours to behold.[4]

Now a few words of caution.

In the biblical or spiritual idiom, visions, 'prophecies', images, never, *never*, deal with social or national projections. They deal always and exclusively with the pilgrim's progress towards enlightenment. They deal with the soul, not the body.

In the biblical idiom, a *city* invariably symbolizes a state of consciousness. A *mountain*—a state of raised consciousness, as in prayer. The *dead or dying people* represent negative thoughts which are "killed off" by (if need be, symbolically, a hail of arrows or bullets) our prayers. The *martyrs* are usually the witnesses, the remaining thoughts or concepts, which are worth preserving. The sprinkling with the blood of martyrs symbolizes the inkling of truth, the influx of spiritual knowledge. The fact that bishops, priests and nuns "died one after the other" gives us some indication of what symbols the unconscious suggests represent that which we should let die within us, within our consciousness. Perhaps they represent dogmatic thoughts, old, tired concepts, rigid, unbending insistence on infallibility. Perhaps we should beware of those among us who attempt to convert all visions into fundamentalist, material, physical images. That is not what the Christ did. His kingdom was not of this world.

***

200627

[Since writing this essay, Cardinal Joseph Ratzinger has been elected to lead the faithful as Pope Benedict XVI. An interesting choice…then other Popes came and went…]

COMMENTS

(1). The nun shared her vision with her two siblings, Francisco and Jacinta in 1917.

(2). The third vision has been recently "released" by the Vatican with a 43-page commentary!

(3). ...now taken for granted that it was the Holy Father, presumably as the only bishop dressed in white; there is no mention of any other identifying marks. (At the time—still the Venerable Pope John Paul II)

(4). Most of the data actual for this essay have been gathered from a report by Reuter in Vatican City, as published by the Gazette, in Montreal on Tuesday, June 27, 2000

*What does a fish know about the water
in which he swims all his life?*

Albert Einstein
[in THE WORLD AS I SEE IT, 1935]

7

ONE ON ONE

There are many that desire to sway the masses. Their need for fame, perhaps power, their need to influence others is a driving force within their nature. It is often recognized as the mark of greatness. I think of it as a great weakness. Throughout the ages, the sages, prophets, saviors, addressed us on a one-on-one basis. They never attempted to either sway or save the masses; always individuals within those masses. Likewise, when they attempted to describe complexion of the "last days" that any particular unit of consciousness, a soul, will undergo in the final stages of its liberation, it is always limited to the experiences of an individual entity.

And more than that.

No one ever succeeded in imparting knowledge on another person, let alone on the masses. All that anyone can do is to stir the desire within one's neighbor to delve into the fount of enlightenment deep within his or her own being. If it were otherwise, the great Masters of the past would have long elevated every one of us to their own illustrious heights. And this brings us to the prophets and their prophecies.

All prophecies describe individual journeys of an individual soul. The apocalyptic events always describe the process of liberation from our material consciousness. The end of the world is the end of your and my transient,

subjective world. The end of a nation is the end of our present system of thoughts, the end of an erroneous mindset.[1] The Higher Consciousness within us is indestructible. Thus, we cannot lose It. What we will lose, ultimately, is the false assumptions, the false idols to which we pay homage in our present mindset. It may take a day, a year, a millennium or a billion years, but each one of us will cross the pearly gates. The gates are eternal. They can wait.
So can we. If we must.
But we don't have to...

There are seers, who claim that our future is like a course of a river which, if we rise high enough, we can see and therefore foretell. Not so. Our life, nevertheless, can be compared to a river. In the beginning, at our very primitive stages, our river cuts a predetermined course through the garden of life. But then, as our consciousness develops, we begin to be faced with diverse possibilities. We become as an effluence swelling into a broad delta, even as the mighty Ganges, on the way to joining with the ocean of Love. Suddenly we are faced with countless opportunities to accelerate or delay our progress. The seer can predict the destination, but not the diverse courses that our life can take to get there. The prophet can describe the many tribulations, but not the intricacies of an individual unfolding. There is always that ever-present principle of uncertainty.
This principle is called, free will.

The past may be fixed, the future, however, can be proposed but not frozen. Since the days of pretentious dogma and assumed infallibility, the principle of uncertainty comes to the fore in every walk of life. It is discernible, under a different guise, in a broad spectrum of disciplines. We find it in the new science of fractals, in the projections of global weather patterns, in medical diagnoses, and even in "the greatest mystery of them all", the quantum mechanics.
At each moment in time every human being (let alone humanity) enjoys an incredible number of choices. We can,

based on his or her previous behavior, project *probable* future, but not insist on it. I recall the behavior of some people during the Second World War. People of reputedly no moral fiber, of any proven strength of character, no backbone—became heroes, both in physical and moral sense. The opposite was also true. The shining examples of the society, the paragons of virtue, stooped and degraded themselves by becoming *folksdeutch*, quislings, they sank below the acceptable level of humanity.

We cannot tell what tomorrow will bring.

What the innumerable scriptural prophecies describe is the *process* of becoming. Such is also analyzed in the Revelation of John.[2] Yet even those who admit to the symbolic nature of prophecies cling to the premise that the prophecies apply on a worldly scale. They seem to harbor a need to know the future, forgetting the fact that only the unknown is dear to the soul.

It is the unknown that is our greatest gift. It is the gift that guaranties us total, absolute, indeed divine, freedom.

Let us enjoy it.

The Revelation of John offers us sweeping insights into our individual unknowns. Each one of us shall unfold in a specific, particular way, but at a certain point in our evolution we shall follow the chart staked out by John. We may not meet all the challenges at once. We may approach the crossroads many a time only to take the wrong fork. But we shall all continue to try and try again until we shall all succeed. Every one of us. For, in a strange, enigmatic yet comforting way, it is not up to us. Most of us still tend to think of ourselves as beings of flesh and blood, endowed with considerable command over our futures, our 'physical' destiny.

Think again!

Our free will is an attribute of our spiritual, not physical life or consciousness. Not of our ego. Physiologically, we are slaves to the laws of the material universe. Physically, we are mobile robots designed to duplicate our DNA. We are made up of atoms that are 99.99% empty space. As for being 'solid', we are little more than bags of water held together by a variety of electro-magnetic attractions, endowed with a minute degree of self-awareness. That's our flesh and blood...

We have a long way to go, but when we finally meet our particular Armageddon, we shall know what to expect. Let's hope we take the right fork.

***
001101

FOOTNOTES

(1). In the scriptures, *nations* symbolize thought patterns. [Refer to my DICTIONARY OF BIBLICAL SYMBOLISM [Inhousepress, Montreal 2001; now available as an ebook.]

(2). Refer to the following essay: *Armageddon*

Future is the hardest thing to predict.

Mark Twain

8

ARMAGEDDON

These-days, there is a marvelous way to make money. A prolific writer, Stephen King, raised it to perfection. You scare the living daylights out of your listener, reader, viewer, and he or she is bound to come back for more. And more. And more. The greater the calamity the better. The more gore, suffering, torture, sadism and death—the more fun. Bullets flying, airplanes smashing, buildings falling, earthquakes shaking, meteors crushing... there is no end to this fun!

Such is the nature of our species.

Sometime in the late sixteenth century it became fashionable to practice this art of intimidation, of making money out of human desire to be scared. A particular example stands out. In the year 1555 the first edition of the *Centuries* appeared. From that date till 1942, in France alone, there have been no less than 60 publications attempting to scare people into believing in the relevancy, or the imminence of the prophesies of Nostradamus.[1] During those four centuries, little (accidents will happen) if anything came true. Many attempted to update the prognostications to align them with the events of the day, only to be replaced by later speculators trying to make money by further updating the dubious relevancy to their present actuality.

Then, for a short while, the age of reason prevailed. The delirious ranting of the Gauls waned, only to be resurrected as a new hobby (of scaring people witless) by using the Good Ol' Bible. In 1967, a self-proclaimed biblical scholar named Herbert W. Armstrong took it upon himself to actualize the

Biblical prophecies. He was so well rewarded for his efforts that he not only succeeded in the creation of his own Church but, thanks to his astute perspicacity, the erudite Armstrong rode to work in his private Rolls-Royce.[2] Unfortunately, his need for imminence forced him to announce that "some 90 percent of all prophecy actually pertains to this latter half of the twentieth century." And furthermore: "These prophecies could not pertain to any time previous to our precarious present!"[3] Alas, we have reached the 21-century and....

Never mind.

Even more baleful is the interpretation of the biblical prophecies by the Jehovah Witnesses. According to them, the world came to an untimely end some years ago.

And then we have the wonderful man, Edgar Cayce, the Sleeping Prophet. He has been instrumental in healing thousands of people, but... the moment his followers attempted to adjust his prophecies to a chronological time-frame, all was lost. At least, Cayce never blamed the Bible for his prophetic contribution. To the best of my knowledge, virtually none of his "prophecies" came true. And Edgar Cayce was a true healer, a very gifted man. Why wouldn't his 'prophecies' work?

Yet the first prize in the biblical department must go to Hal Lindsey.[4] In his book: *The 1980's Countdown to Armageddon* he managed to scare enough people to waste enough money to keep his book for "over 20 weeks on the New York times bestseller list." Luckily for us, in his introduction, the man who *"During the last 25 years* (has) *been studying prophecy,"* wrote that: *"The decade of 1980s could very well be the last decade of history as we know it."* (Whatever that means!)

Well, the 1980s are over, the 1990s are over, and... I can only presume the "countdown" goes on. And on. And on...

[In parenthesis I wish to repeat my thesis regarding the marvelous way of making money from scaring people. On the cover of Lindsey's book mentioned above, incidentally published in 1981, there is a list of five other literary jewels, all related to our impending (past) demise. It's enough to scare me witless. How about you?]

While most prognosticators make full use of the Revelation of St. John, (known to the Catholics as the Apocalypse) to advance their sinister theses, the representatives of the Vatican prefer to ride their favorite horse of carrot and the stick.[5] Rather than concentrating on the prophetic aspect of the Revelation, they assure us that the purpose of John's vision was *inter alia*, to assure *"God's intervention in judgment bringing punishment upon those afflicting the members of his Church."* For reasons of their own, the church scholars diligently ignore the biblical assurance that "The Father (God) judges no man."[6] Further, we are consoled and reassured that *"Hell exists as the punishment not only for evil spirits but for evildoers among men."*[7] This inane interpretation carries the full power of the Roman church, the *Nihil obstat* of the *Censor deputatus*[8], and the *Imprimatur* of the Bishop. However, while the church does not stoop to fundamentalist prophetic cataclysms, it does assure us that in John's magnificent vision of our individual unfoldment *"no new truths are promulgated..."* Alas, certainly not in the Catholic interpretation.

In spite of any and/or all of the above, people seem bent on indolent wallowing in the scary interpretations of biblical and/or any other prophecies. No matter how many examples I would cite of the innocuous quality of their vitriolic raving, people would still search out the scariest scenarios, as long as such would not touch them personally.

Alas, there's the rub.

All, ALL, biblical prophecies are intensely and exclusively personal, which is precisely why people feel compelled to depersonalize them, to push them away, reject their own inevitable futures. This psychotic role-reversal substituting "them" for "us" leads to obvious consequences. In this revised scenario, the Revelation of Saint John provides the scaremongers of doomsday synopsis with greatest source of ammunition. There, they really flourish. The revelation is replete with falling stars, bottomless pits exuding smoke, chariots of many horses running into battle, pillars of fire, thousands slain, and all this dressed-up in fire and brimstone and begging to be taken literally by exploiters of the human weakness for depraved sensationalism.

The late Armstrong mentioned above, went a step further. Fired no doubt by the flamboyant poetry of Saint John, he as good as equates the Vatican with the great whore of the Revelation. Yet no part of the Revelation has anything to do with any organization, past or present, other than how we organize our thoughts. The red whore symbolizes our emotional nature, even as the beast of the Apocalypse stands for the depth of our subconscious mind, wherein our materiality has been anchored for millions of years. After all, we became aware of our spiritual nature (if now) only recently. But evolution created our subconscious as the storehouse of data necessary for our *physical* survival. To change our orientation from material to spiritual, from being (spiritually) dead to consciously Alive, we must dig deep and destroy our lower nature. And only then the new, childlike consciousness can be born within our hearts, and when It first manifests Its presence, we must protect It. We must take It into the desert, where no "old ways" will endanger Its development. It is a precious child. "For unto us a child is born... and his name is Wonderful..."[9] But first we must win our final battle with our lower nature. This and only this is the Armageddon. This and only this is the final battle spoken of by St. John, by Ezekiel, Daniel and others.

We can deny it all we want, but the future of the world is not only unknown, but also unknowable. There are as many possibilities, as many directions human evolution might take, as there are individualization's of Soul in the endless cosmos. Or as many as there are stars in the sky.

And... just think, we are all immortal. The stars are not.

***

001103

FOOTNOTES

(1). The various protagonists are listed by James Laver in NOSTRADAMUS (or Future Foretold) [Collins Publ., London 1942]

(2). The Worldwide Church of God.

(3). Armstrong, Herbert W., THE UNITED STATES AND BRITAIN IN PROPHECY, [Worldwide Church of God 1967]

(4). I already had the dubious pleasure to ostracize Mr. Lindsey on one previous occasion. It should be noted, however, that Mr. Lindsay sates the needs of many neurotic people.

(5). Heidt, William G., O. S. B., THE BOOK OF THE APOCALYPSE [The Liturgical Press, Collegeville, Minnesota 1962]

(6). John 5:20.

(7). ibid.: Introduction, item 8.

(8). I understand this to be the office of the Holy (?) Inquisition.

(9). Isaiah 9:6

We have now reached a stage in the history of the world when the whole of the human race as a body, or at lest a large majority of people of every kind and of every race, are ready for the second coming of the Christ...

It is beginning to happen... (it) is taking place now in the hearts of hundreds of thousands of people.

Emmet Fox, *The Second Coming of the Christ*,
DIAGRAMS FOR LIVING
[Harper and Row, 1968; pg.157.]

9
THE ERRANT SUPERMAN

On occasion, we tend to blame the Superman we call Lord, or God, for having created us with certain infirmities, shortcomings, gradually dilapidating bodies. How and why does God permit such evils, ills, sicknesses, death itself? We never seem to stop to wonder that it took millions of years to create, or evolve, our present physiques together with our inquisitive intellect and emotional responsive nature to a level when we can even ask such questions. Not to mention to be able to just be, should we choose to be, self-sufficient.

While our bodies can be described as fantastically advanced biological machines, the same cannot be said of our minds, let alone our emotional make-up. If we, humans, were able to produce a robot, an android (or any of the artificial intelligences populating the realm of science-fiction), which approached the complexity of our own physical enclosures, we would be in position to criticize evolution (the God's workshop) for our physiological shortcomings. Yet, while we are progressively more adept at sending men to the moon, we are still quite unable to so much as create, or put together, a single drop of amino acid, the very basic building block of biological life. Sometimes we forget that our bodies are first and foremost factories for the reproduction of amino acids. Later, much later we became host for the selfish gene, the consequences of which still leads us to claim superiority over other life forms, other genes, although we had nothing whatever to do with the creation of either.[1] Physically our genes can be said to be at the base of our instinct of self-preservation. Unbeknownst to us, we, the hosts, the biological production lines, will guide and stimulate us to destroy whatever might threaten our own species' survival. Such is the role of the selfish gene.

Our minds, therefore, have not risen, as yet, to the most elementary level of being able to create a single molecule of biological life. We have developed substantial competence in destroying life-forms other than ours (see below), but not to replace them with anything better. We are killers by nature, since nature made us killers. We deny this on a sunny day, but come periods of trials, of circumstances threatening our survival, and our true nature comes to the fore. Homo sapiens survived because we became proud members of the omnivora, and indeed, in times of stress the human animal will eat everything. Including each other. And kill to do so. Indiscriminately.

As for our emotional make-up, it also has its roots in our physical nature. Only now we not only kill in order to survive, but because we enjoy it. I know people who can hardly think of more fun than to go hunting, to shoot ducks or deer, birds and animals of such beauty, of such biological wonder, as to surpass any and every thing man ever was or is capable of creating. No matter—killing is fun. I watched the faces of my dear friends performing the senseless carnal act of slaughter on the innocent, defenseless animals. We, after millions of years of evolution, have learned to derive pleasure from the destruction of that which has never done us any harm. Yet should a hungry animal attack us to feed its young, we call it a wild beast, a carnivorous monster, a primitive creature. Are we any better? We certainly are better at killing!

Only at killing.

And that's not all. We not only vent our emotional frustrations on the murder of the innocents of other species, but we wage wars on our own kind. We indulge in mass slaughter of the males and females of our own species; we murder our young, our helpless—the unresisting. We call it collateral damage. We don't even eat our victims' bodies, but leave the cadavers to rot as evidence of our primitive nature.

So why should the Superman (God, or whatever you want to call the evolutionary force) have given us more than we already have? Why should evolution proceed to enhance the miracle of our bodies to make us live even longer, to enhance our immune system that we might survive the ever-harsher attacks from viral or bacterial invasions? Should that happen, we would, in our folly, overpopulate the world even more. We would wage even more wars to gain ground for our particular gene variant that it might reproduce itself for our pride and glory. And the greatest killers among us would be decorated with DKC's, the Distinguished Killing Crosses and shining MM's or Murdering Medals awarded for the greatest number of kills of other mobile gene carriers. We would hang these trinkets, proudly, on our meager chests; meager because technology would provide us with the means and ability to kill with killing gadgets, from a distance, impersonally. The days are long gone when we didn't shoot till we saw the whites of our enemies' eyes.

Once, machines had been intended as the extensions of our dreams, our aspirations. Today we are the extensions of our machines. We are envious, resentful biological robots. Little more than genetic production factories. Perhaps that is all we are.

Unless...

Unless there is more to us than just our minds, emotions and self-replicating ability. Unless there is more to life than physical survival, than slaughter and gluttony, than living at the expense of the weaker species which we did not, and could not even attempt to create.

Unless we are still more than biological entities of such astounding, magnificent complexity. Could it be that we are supposed to take over our reproductive machines with all their built-in survival traits and turn them to different pursuit, reaching beyond physical continuance. Perhaps, just perhaps, we might then have the right to call ourselves a superior race, a superior species.

Or, perhaps, only then we shall realize that we are not superior. That at the very ground of being we are all one.

We might realize, then, that every time we kill we commit a protracted suicide, a slow depreciation of our potential. Killing is in our nature. We must kill in order to survive. We must eat or be eaten. Survival of our genes is built into our primitive psyche. Isn't it time we rose above it? Isn't it time we suspended our biological urges to find out whom or what is it that we are replicating?

Isn't it time we made an effort to find out who we really are?

There is one single spark of hope in our depravity. There is no reason, absolutely no reason to suppose that the evolution of the human species has reached its end. So let us give the Superman a little more time in his heavenly workshop. We can hope, we *must* hope, that during the next few million, perchance billion, years, some of us shall grow to be less primitive than we are now. Perhaps then we shall stop blaming the Superman for our foibles, and begin to take responsibility for our actions. Or, if we don't like this idea, we might try doing better ourselves.

We shall see. If... we survive.

I put my money on the Superman.

***

001112

FOOTNOTES

(1). The term "selfish gene" had been coined by Richard Dawkins who wrote a book by this title

10

BLOOD BATH

[This essay has been previously published in a number of magazines]

According to Mr. Moore, a gentleman of literary aspirations otherwise unknown to me, we, Canadians, indulge in an annual blood bath. No, not the slaughter of the millions of cows and calves, pigs and piglets, fowl and fish and whatever else serves to distend our obese paunches, but of "pre-born" children.[1] Until recently, the adjectives "pre-born" or "un-born", or "un-dead" have been reserved for ghouls, the living-dead adorning our Halloween horror films. Now we are told that children have joined such grotesque ranks. Albeit, thankfully, only the pre-born variety. It seems evident that Mr. Moore and his "pro-life" compadres, would like to make abortion illegal, probably under the penalty of death. The fundamentalists like the penalty of death. History has shown that the "pro-lifers" love killing those who disagree with them. Thankfully, according to the pool which he quotes, Canadians do not share this sentiment.

The same cannot be said for mother nature.

Another recent article reprinted from the Washington Post has announced the results of an extensive scientific research which states that: *"Most newly conceived human embryos harbor colossal genetic defects that are incompatible with life."* Furthermore, *"...most pregnancies—whether naturally occurring or the result of test-tube fertilization—quietly fail within days or a few weeks after conception."*[2] It seems that we have no choice but to make mother nature illegal. Moreover, it is quite apparent that Mr.

Moore has not been recently pregnant and thus does not speak from first hand experience of multiple spontaneous abortions, even though they contribute to a blood-bath infinitely greater than the one to which he is referring. No one in their right mind would question the thesis that life begins at conception. It may be wiser, however, to refer to this *life* as *biological life*. Such as is abundantly manifest in *all* animals, fowl and fish which, I presume, Mr. Moore together with the rest of the human race have no qualms in slaughtering in order to masticate them in vastly excessive quantities. The problem, I suggest, rests in the excess, not in the fact *per se*. Strangely though it may seem, Jesus of Nazareth is said to have eaten meat, while Adolf Hitler was a vegetarian. Perhaps this is one reason why the "pro-lifers" argue that they are regarded by the "pro-choicers"[3] as *"just a bunch of lunatic fringe religious fanatics who need not be taken seriously."* Quite true. Perhaps this well earned opinion would change if the "pro-lifers" would desist from on-going murder of millions of animals of all species, or define how does the human animal differ from the remaining fauna. The question remains, therefore, whether we draw any distinction between human and non-human life. If there is a difference, then the question is *at which point* in the biological life does this difference occur.

The sausage-shaped globs of DNA, known as chromosomes, carry practically all the genes inside a cell. Most human cells contain 46 chromosomes of which only 23 from each parent are passed on at impregnation. Has life already begun? Are the residual chromosomes murdered? There are *millions* of them.
The slaughter gets worse.
Compared to the other mammals, humans are very inefficient reproducers. Only about one-in-four of natural monthly attempts result in pregnancy. Are the products of unsuccessful attempts murdered? The eggs have been impregnated, but *sensitive hormone test have also shown that a high percentage of early pregnancies end within days or a*

few weeks.[4] Nature is really selective. Whatever she doesn't like, she aborts. For a time, the human embryos hover on the brink of molecular self-destruction. Then, after a perilous beginning, some achieve genetic stability, and continue their growth. Some become babies. *Born* babies.[5]

Perhaps in another few million years evolution will improve her batting average. Perhaps we can help nature in her quest. But please, don't make nature illegal just because she protects our biological integrity by an ongoing, continuous "blood-bath".

We still haven't defined if, and if so when, the human life becomes different from the rest of fauna. If we claim a different status from the rest of animal kingdom, if we do not abide by the kill-or-be-killed dictum for food, for territory, for power, then I see little or no evidence of it. We certainly murder a great many more of our own species than any other mammal. And kill not just our "pre-born", but also the well and truly and very selectively born children, as well as our adults and our hapless elderly. We murder them indiscriminately, individually and *en masse*, often without rancor. We then adorn the chests of our most successful murderers with colorful ribbons, elevate them to the ranks of heroes, build statues for them, put their unaffected faces on postage stamps. We are really proud of them. We forget that the genes in those murdered *do not differ in any way* from the genes, which our parents have passed on to us. We murder because, as I've already written in the previous essay on *The Errant Supermen*, we like murdering. It is in our blood. It is carried in our genes.

Except in those few who kill no more.

***

001113

[This essay has been published a number of times…]

FOOTNOTES

(1). Moore, Charles W. *A sense of betrayal*, The Gazette, Montreal Nov.13th, 2000
(2). Weiss, Rick: Embryo study shows defects are killers, The Gazette, Montreal, Oct.23rd, 2000
(3). These are people who hate the waste of a human embryo but do not take it upon themselves to tell women what to do with their bodies.
(4). Weiss, Rick, ibid.
(5). It may be of some interest, that at the time of writing, the Internet offered 470 pages on the subject of abortion. The matter is not likely to be resolved in our lifetime.

What on earth do I think that I myself am?
Or you?...
We roam the world looking for the raw materials needed to assemble the parts needed to maintain ourselves and eventually assemble another robot capable of the same feats.

Richard Dawkins
CLIMBING MOUNT IMPROBABLE
[W.W. Norton & Co., New York, 1966; p. 281]

11

ETERNITY

Many religious leaders assure us that should we manage to behave ourselves, we have a good chance to be rewarded with a permanent residence in heaven. There, according to those aspiring theologians, we shall shed all worries, forsake all ills, rise above all evil, all pain and suffering. We shall also terminate all efforts, give up strife and striving, content ourselves to just be. Like gods. Eternal, unchanging, unfeeling, indifferent. Being integral to That which is All Knowing, we would lose all interest of discovery. Being above and beyond human emotions or intellect, we would neither feel nor think. Being integral to Love Itself, we would no longer merely love someone. Having all, we would desire nothing... basking in the Eternal Light of Eternal Intelligence, devoid of personality, of friends or enemies, ever unconcerned. We shall have reached the desireless state of Being.

For ever.

Think about it again. We shall spend eternity in a state of Being, relishing our immortality. We shall perhaps retain a vague awareness of our individuality, of an individuality we once had, perhaps enjoyed, but mostly we shall be immersed within the Ocean from which we once emerged. We shall enjoy the inexplicable Bliss of Being. This is what heaven is all about. It is about having one's Being in abundant Bliss.

On and on... and on... Forever.

For Eternity.

Eternity is a very, very long time...

Are you sure this is what you want?

If God is so happy just Being, and surely God IS, why did He (She, It) create man? Or better still—the world? Or even more so, why did God create the evolutionary process, which led, under His omniscient guidance, to an entity through which, eventually, He found a mode of being endowed with self-awareness?

Or is it *the mode of Becoming?*

I have written before, as have many seekers of Reality, that God has no being other than through a *mode* of being. It now seems, that if we are one such mode, then we, locked into the state of continuous becoming can offer but this mode to our Creator. It seems that in heaven God IS. On earth, and surely God is omnipresent, God shares in our mode of Becoming. At least for six days out of seven we, humans, provide this mode. Some, who wish or can, may attempt to take Sunday or Saturday off to merge into a state of being, but the rest of the time we are busy becoming.

Surely, this is as it should be.

We are given all the equipment to improve this earthly condition. While in heaven or on Sunday, we may enjoy rest, detachment; but our reason for being here, on earth, is to improve and continue improving the mode of becoming. And unless we are prepared to give up the joys of conquest, of self-discovery (for all discovery is, in a sense, *self-discovery*), of manifesting Love through loving, of manifesting Intelligence, Creativity, through all forms of activity, we must remain on Earth. Or some other planet. Or on planets of billions upon billions of other stars, swirling within billions upon billions of other galaxies, perhaps within countless other universes. But ever becoming. For ever providing the euphoric joy of being instruments of the Infinite Love, Infinite Intelligence, Infinite Life.

Worlds without end.

Do you still want heaven as your permanent, eternal abode?

I once wrote an essay on *Being and Becoming*.[1] It now seems that I must expand my understanding of our modes of being. Isn't this what life is all about? To grow in understanding? I remember my friend's frustration when she cried: "It's too late to agree with me, I've changed my mind!" I still hold that successful contemplation enables us to become one with the object of our attention. It enables us to merge with the Essence of our Being, to lose our identity within the Ocean of our origin. But...

But now it seems to me that, when it happens, when we succeed in stepping out the constrains of time and space, when time comes to a stop hovering for a blissful instant on the fringe of Eternity, and when we experience ultimate Oneness, then such an instant is a reward for providing the Infinite Consciousness with a willing vehicle through which It too might enjoy the mode of Becoming.

Forever.

For although ever is a very, very long continuance, Eternity is but an instant beyond temporal duration.

***

001115

FOOTNOTES

(1). Kapuscinski, Stanislaw BEYOND RELIGION Volume I. [Inhousepress, Montreal 1997, 2001; Amazon Kindle Edition, 2010]

12

VISUAL PERCEPTION

In the *Introduction* to this collection of essays I mentioned the futility of reliance on our senses to determine the reality in which we find ourselves. Here I would like to examine the matter in some greater detail. As the subject could fill volumes, I shall limit myself to a brief discussion of the visual perception only.

Our eyes are sensitive to photons.

Photons are quanta (groupings or bunches) of electromagnetic energy. The vast range of the electromagnetic waves includes, *inter alia,* X rays, gamma rays, radio and television waves as well as what we know as light. The waves range from lengths greater than the diameter of the earth to others so short that a billion strung together would barely span the width of your fingernail. Sandwiched between the lengthy infrared and the extremely short ultraviolet waves is the visible spectrum ranging from violet through blue, green, yellow and orange to red. This tiny portion of the visible spectrum varies in lengths from 0.000076 centimeters at the red end of the visible spectrum to 0.000038 centimeters at the violet end.[1] While our bodies are affected by various waves of electromagnetic energy, our eyes recognize only this tiny amplitude. Until the year 1800, man has known no other photons. To this day, all other photons remain invisible (to the naked eye).

There is a good reason for this.

Many of us think that human vision operates on principles similar to a camera: we take a picture and store it in memory for later use. This is true only in part. The human retina is not a uniform surface. Only an area about one-third of a millimeter in diameter can absorb information in great detail. This area contains special light-sensitive cells. The rest of the retina transmits impressions of whole groups of cells, and this offers much less detail. Only about one-hundredth of visual field can absorb an image with any precision. Thus though a single glance offers us an *impression*, thousands of co-ordinated eye movements, up and down and sidewise, are required to scan a landscape or a painting in any detail.

Then (simultaneously) we must transfer this information to the section of the cortex, about two inches square, at the back of the head, through the optic nerve consisting of about one million fibers of rods and cones. While the transmission is continuous the individual impulses last a tenth of a second. Rather like a film projection on a cinema screen (giving impression of continuous movement), or of light being continuous from electric bulb connected to an alternating current (AC). Finally, all the information fed to the cortex must be made available to the rest of the brain for cognition. Yet, if there were a direct neural connection between the million visual fibers and the ten-thousand-million of neurons of the rest of the brain, our cranium would boil.[2] It would also fill a very large house. Enough said that nature had to compromise—again.

Now imagine the range which our retinas can detect being extended beyond the tiny spectrum. The least we can say that the human race would sport extremely large heads. Thus it seems that from the point of view of visual perception, the human race has already reached the limit of its evolutionary development. And yet...

And yet the saints, the mystics, the spiritual masters report of such beauty as to be completely beyond the perception of mere mortals. Is there a different way of looking altogether? Do the spiritual masters know something we don't? Or perhaps there is something akin to spiritual eyes, spiritual vision, which reaches far and beyond the one million fibers of our visual nerve, beyond the one-third of a millimeter of our ultra-sensitive retina. Or is it a matter of chemistry as implied by Aldous Huxley after he experimented with mescaline, or as proposed in the teaching that Don Juan offered to Castaneda.[3]

From the pure physicist's point of view, things get even worse. There is the red and ultraviolet shift recorded by our instruments aimed at stars and galaxies gallivanting in our night sky. It seems that the colors we observe are affected by the velocity and the direction of travel of the object observed.

And then the visual perception is subject to the "Rayleigh scattering", so named after Lord Rayleigh. He determined that when sunlight strikes even the clearest, the most 'pure' earth atmosphere, it is still scattered. The visible (as well as the invisible) sunlight consists of photons, which strike the molecules of mainly nitrogen and oxygen (likewise quite invisible to the human eye) that are suspended in the atmosphere. As the photons hit these molecules they bounce off. Lord Rayleigh observed that the short wavelengths, those on the blue end of the spectrum, are scattered and/or bounced away by the air molecules more efficiently than long wavelengths. In layman's language this means that blue light is scattered much better than the red light. It is this predisposition towards that scattering effect of the blue light that makes our skies blue.[4]

In a like vein, any man, any intelligent being that could disperse photons in this range would be invisible to the human eye. Perhaps this goes some way to explain how Jesus managed to disappear unharmed from the Temple in Jerusalem, or how Sai Baba, today, seemingly manages to be in two places at once.

But whatever the implications of the 'secret' knowledge that the great men of past (and present) possessed, one fact is beyond argument. We must never forget that the magic of today is the science of tomorrow. In our search for truth, we cannot rely (exclusively) on our visual senses. The same is true of our other physical endowments, which, while serving us well within the realm of becoming, are of little use in, what man always referred to as the Higher Realms. What man doesn't seem to realize, is that the Higher Realms are coexistent with the realm we live in. They are but higher states of consciousness.

***

001120

FOOTNOTES

(1). Gleamed from Walter, W. Grey THE LIVING BRAIN, [Pelican Books, 1961]. The number of fibers required would be in the order of $10^6 \times 10^{10}$ or 10,000,000,000,000,000.

(2). Huxley, Aldous THE DOORS OF PERCEPTION and HEAVEN AND HELL [Penguin Books 1957]; and Castaneda, Carlos, THE TEACHING OF DON JUAN, A SECOND REALITY et al. [Simon and Shuster]

(3). Gleamed from THE COSMIC CONNECTION by Carl Sagan (produced by Jerome Agel) [Dell publ., New York, 1973.]

(4). A GLIMPSE OF NOTHINGNESS, [Washington Square Press, New York 1978] pg.183

*We are frightened of the emptiness within and try to fill it.
With ideas, with names, and definitions.*

> *Janwillem van de Wetering*
> A GLIMPSE OF NOTHINGNESS,
> [Washington Square Press, New York 1978; pg.183]

13

EUTHANASIA

Political, scientific and religious fundamentalists, people determined to maintain *status quo*, invariably search for a yes or no answer. They yearn for dogmas and are themselves staunchly dogmatic. There are, of course, exceptions but, for the most part, their world is black and white, devoid of shades and nuances, devoid of color, potential for growth. They think they know all the answers. If not themselves then their betters: priests, imams, icons in power, leaders of their society. Such people obviously express a need for stability, a hunger for reliability in a world they find confusing, unpredictable often capricious.

These unfortunates seem unaware that change is the quintessence of life.

And all this in spite of countless scientific observations pointing to a reality that exhibits attributes, which are invariably contingent, provisory and interdependent on all other data collected. It is as though the Theory of Relativity imposed its laws on the whole universe, on countless billions of galaxies, on the entire God's manifestation, but could be ignored in everyday life.

Not so.

If we are to learn through the gift of life, then we must accept that the only aspect of the future that is guaranteed is that tomorrow will be different from today. Even though history appears to repeat itself, it does so in different shades, with different overtones, offering us ever-new opportunities to learn, to rise, and to expand our horizons. And history, *the past of the future*, is never black and white.

In my essay on *Suicide* [1], I attempted to show how an attitude toward suicide changes depending on our understanding of who we are. Today we face a new dilemma, or apparent dilemma, which the government of the Netherlands is attempting to solve through legislation. In my today's daily newspaper I've read the following title: *The Doctors in Netherlands have long practiced mercy killing.*[2] Following a debate on the practices of the medical profession over the last 26 years, the Netherlands will be the first country to formally allow mercy killing.[3] The legislation shall have multiple safety factors to protect the "patient" from abuse by the medical profession let alone any members of the patient's family greedily awaiting the inheritance. The foremost precondition is the presence of "unremitting and unbearable suffering." The records indicate that during the course of 1999 Dutch doctors helped 2,216 people to die with dignity, an adjective cherished by the late Mother Theresa, the Pope Jean-Paul II, and trade union leaders alike. One can but wonder what will be the official Vatican's reaction to this courageous legislation. It will prove an onerous decision for an organization which sanctioned selective killing (heretics and suchlike) over many centuries.[4]

And this brings us, again, to the heart of the matter.

Are we our bodies, be they healthy or contorted in agony, or are we more than biological constructs, which are all too often subjected to such undignified terminal treatment. Medicine met much greater success in extending life than extending the *quality* of life. Until the equation changes, we must answer a number of vital questions. We must decide whether it is 'I' who is degraded by an incurable disease, or is it merely my body. Am 'I' and my body one-and-the-same? Is any person unaware (not *yet* aware) of his *true* nature really human?[5] Or is he or she an animal in whom humanity, the divine spark, is still a*waiting to be born*. Or even more, can our humanity be lost under certain unbearable conditions? If we release the spirit, the consciousness, from a body contorted by agonizing pain—a body subjected to such suffering that it looses all perception of anything other than pain—are we in contravention of the commandment Thou shalt not kill?

It seems reasonable to assume that pain, ugliness, mental or moral deprivation never originate with God, and that we should assist in the elimination of such aberrations in any manner possible. But should we do so even at the risk of terminating biological functions? If in principle we answer yes, then the only conditions that would apply would be those that assure that such an assistance neither would nor could be abused.

It is my contention, that ultimately there is only one reason to maintain biological life: to serve as channel for Higher Consciousness. If, for example, the intensity of pain precludes or distorts such a possibility, the purpose of being human is lost. We can never be absolutely sure if and when such a moment occurs, but we have developed a brain, an ability to think, and we are obliged to use this ability with discretion. Contrary to many well-meaning martyr-masochists, religious or otherwise, suffering for the sake of suffering is the antithesis of love, of wisdom, of mercy, of commons sense, and—surely—of divine intent.

In the relativistic world, neither life nor death are black or white. They affect every one of us differently. We are, after all, individualizations of One Soul—of Single Consciousness. Perhaps we should refrain from legislating life or death. If, through an act of our will, we allow our bodies to have children, perhaps we should also be in position to allow our bodies to die. Our *own* bodies, *not* other peoples'. With or without assistance. With or without legislation. Surely, we should never refuse help when asked, especially when asked by the sick and suffering. Whatever that request might be. Perhaps we really shouldn't pass judgment, especially on the sick and suffering. Can anyone decide for another when he or she feels no longer representing the image and likeness of God?

What we should legislate is peoples' right to practice their divine gift of Free Will. It is the only way to learn. There is none other.

***
001126

FOOTNOTES

(1). BEYOND RELGION Vol.I. [Inhousepress Montreal 1997, 2001, Amazon Kindle 2010]
(2). Reported by Reuters, the Montreal GAZETTE, Nov. 25, 2000. According to Southam News Service, records of such practice have been kept for 26 years.
(3). The 1996 law which in the Northern Territory of Australia allowed medically assisted suicide for the terminally ill was later repealed.
(4). As well as conversions at the point of a sword, crusades, inquisition, valedictory blessings of armies on the eve of battle, etc..
(5). Jesus referred to them as dead, as in: "...let the dead bury their dead." Matthew 8:22

When the Ten Thousand things are viewed in their oneness, we return to the Origin and remain where we have always been.

Sen T'sen

14

PROBABILITY

There once was a time when things were simple. People, mostly priesthood, knew exactly how the world worked. They knew that the earth was the center of the universe, God ruled all things: people, animals, and what-have-you, in a strong albeit benevolent fashion. If you were good you went to heaven, bad—to hell, lukewarm (if Catholic)—to purgatory. There was hardly any concern with any aspect of free will, in fact the less the better. According to most religions, free will was one of God's major blunders. We were meant to be guided, led by the hand, nose if necessary, slowly, diligently, purposefully, for our own good.

Those were the days!

At that time, things had been simple. There was earth (mostly flat) and there was heaven (always up and strictly after death). There was matter and there was spirit. Spirit was good; matter was bad, evil. There was God (good) and there was the Devil (bad). Two powerful, opposing forces.

And then man ate an apple and started thinking.

What if things aren't so simple? What if the earth isn't the center of the world? What if we determined our own futures? What if good and evil are all mixed up, blended, and hard to unwind? What if...?

Then problems started in earnest.

Aeons passed with man wandering the dessert. Starved of infallible guidance, relying on an evolving brain, yet not advanced enough do him much good. He tried a million different directions. Knowledge accumulating in his subconscious gradually assured the survival of his species. His genes grew stronger, his mind... often weaker. Survival of the species became *sine qua non dictum* (only Latin hadn't been invented yet so man didn't know what it meant). Men tried going back to the old ways, to good and evil, to God and the Devil. Some still do. Wars had started; the Devil seemed to prevail in many areas of life. Things got from bad to worse.

Whatever happened to Eden where all was so very, very... Man forgot what was it that was "so very, very." What was so good about Eden? And then one man remembered.

In Eden there was no good and evil.

The man became known as Buddha and he offered us the middle path.

Neither heaven nor earth, neither good nor evil, just the middle. A narrow path. Rather than good or evil, it offered *bliss*. His near contemporary, Confucius, said that to go beyond is as wrong as to fall short.[1] Five hundred years later, another man offered us peace. His name was Jesus. Paul of Taurus said that the peace Jesus offered passes all understanding. Nobody believed either of them. People preferred war. Wars offered a mix of good and evil. Like in the old ways. The old ways have been (still are) sustained by all the known religions. After all, if there were no good and evil, what would the priests do? Man walking the middle path offends no one. Man at peace does not require absolution. He abides in a state of bliss. He is whole. Holy?

Religions thrive on wars between good and evil.

And what of us, simple folk?

Apparently, most of the time, we are suspended between heaven and earth. Neither good nor evil. Sounds a bit like the middle path. Only the peace is still missing. Why? Perhaps "good" is something else altogether. Perhaps it is neither a thing, nor a feeling nor even an action but a potential. A potential, a predisposition, a tendency to see things in a certain way. Isn't it true that a glass can be half full or half empty? If God is an inexhaustible potential, and the predisposition towards good (thus God) omnipresent, then isn't good omnipresent too? And wouldn't good offer us peace?

Perhaps it's just the definition of good we must change. Perhaps good is not the opposite of evil. Perhaps good has no opposite. It just is. Like God. Omnipresent, filling the interstellar, intergalactic space with predisposition towards good. We might oppose it—*we*, not the devil. We might never be sure of anything but that the predisposition, the probability of good is always there. Everywhere.

It would be enough.

And evil? Evil would be just an imaginary absence of good.

Enter Quantum Mechanics.

The Theory of uncertainty and probability. Quantum Theory tells us that the world is as unknowable as God Himself. We can guess (calculate) what God might want, but we cannot be sure. We can be sure only within a certain probability. And since Quantum theory encompasses the whole universe, then, in a manner of speaking, it encompasses God. The manifested God. Not just the divine mystery within the hearts of Black Holes. Such singularities are beyond the laws of physics, beyond knowableness. They are the domain which God, so far, refuses to reveal to us. They are domains wherein all things are possible, only no one knows what "all" is. Perhaps that is where all matter is converted back to spirit, where new universes are born. Millions or Billions of them. With different laws, different probabilities. We cannot know—the unknowable mystery of Black Holes. According to the leading theoretical physicist, Stephen Hawking, the world is replete with them. All over the space. Rather like God.

One could say that, in terms of probability, nothing describes God and His domain (heaven) better than the Chaos Theory. Like its Quantum sister, Chaos Theory assures us

that although in the ultimate sense chaos is unknowable, it does nevertheless exhibit a predisposition towards a resolution in an orderly fashion. In other words, there is an inherent probability that whatever emerges from chaos carries a predisposition towards order. Towards good. Rather like heaven or God.
Isn't it funny that terms, which heretofore applied only to theology, now, recently, keep cropping up in physics? Makes you wander...

My private world is often in a state of chaos. Perhaps not of the primordial variety, but chaos nevertheless. It used to worry me. Not any more. Now, thanks to the Quantum Theory and the Theory of Chaos, I know that within a high degree of probability, i.e. if I do not interfere too much, my own private world will unfold itself as is should. That whatever happens to me, in my reality, there is a high probability that it will happen for my good. For the good of my world. Sometimes I even feel that I am guided, led by hand, slowly, diligently, purposefully, with incredible patience, for my own good. Perhaps not much has changed, after all. Perhaps we all live in the eternal present.
Somehow this makes me happy.
Very happy, at times.

***
001128

FOOTNOTES

(1). c.551-479? B.C.

Science without religion is lame.
Religion without science is blind.

Albert Einstein

15

WHY THE FALL

History is replete with cataclysmic falls. We have witnessed, or read about, the falls of innumerable kingdoms, of the Third Reich, of the British Empire. Evidently, all monuments to man's pride and glory are transient, ephemeral. Yet only one fall left an indelible mark on everyone of us: The Fall of Man.

This initial fall, described so poetically in the first book of Genesis, is equated with the ignominious expulsion of Adam and Eve from the Garden of Eden. It seems that loss of innocence is the price our forefathers (fore-parents) had to pay for the acquisition of knowledge. "And Lord God said, Behold, the man is become as one of us, to know good and evil..."[1] Man acquired the power of discrimination. Once Eve came into the picture, or into the garden, the 'fall' was inevitable. Not because she seduced Adam with an apple, only because in the biblical idiom Eve represents Adam's *nephesh*, the animal soul, which we know as the subconscious. Without a subconscious Adam could not survive as a thinking entity. Every animal needs a storehouse of knowledge to which it can defer certain functions of survival. And at this stage, Adam was but a primitive animal, only vaguely aware of his subconscious (Eve).

Hardly a fall.

Quite the contrary.

While it is true that the blissful state of Edenic consciousness is to be cherished, it is only in dualistic reality that we can fulfill our purpose. The expulsion from Eden was necessary to enable man to learn of his potential. It is also true that the very awareness of good and evil removes us from the state of blissful inertia. There is no differentiation in Edenic consciousness. All is perfect. But it is not knowledge alone which removes the state of bliss from our consciousness, but rather our apparent inability to commit all our resources to the discovery of our true nature which will lead us back to our true home. No longer as innocent children, but in full knowledge of who we are. This cannot be accomplished without the 'fall'.

What is Edenic consciousness?

It is a condition of accepting reality as we find it. It is rejoicing in the world without necessarily passing judgment on the evidence of our senses. It is living in the present. It is accepting our immortality.

Our *post*-Edenic consciousness is colored by instinct for physical survival. We learn by metabolizing our repeated choices. Once we have chosen to survive as biological entities, this choice became metabolized by our genes. Our subconscious (the mental equivalent of our genes and chromosomes) imposes instinctive reactions to our environment. Whatever is conducive to our (physical) survival we regard as good. We are subliminally threatened by the unknown, by the fear of tomorrow.

At the face of it, Edenic consciousness is not that difficult. Wild animals spend most of their time in Paradise. Compared to us, humans, they demonstrate a relatively carefree life. They do not live in constant fear of danger (when threatened they rely on fright not on fear)[2], they do not worry about tomorrow, they do not accumulate riches or food, destroy other let alone their own species as a preventive measure. Why cannot we act in a similar fashion? Do other animals know something we don't?

Why should we, on occasion, suspend judgment? Judgment is only possible in comparison to something else. Nothing is intrinsically good or bad. Until we pass judgment, a thing, event, or action remains neutral. It is as though we applied Quantum Theory to our everyday life. Until we measure anything, event or whatever, such is suspended in the realm of infinite possibilities, a virtual world not quite invading our mode of existence. Only when we direct attention towards anything, the object of our attention assumes a comparative status. The object enters our reality colored by our subjective observation or judgment.

Thus a knife is neither good nor bad until it cuts bread, serves as an instrument in a surgical operation, or is used to commit murder. When an indifferent item is connected to an act, it assumes the quality of that act, it is graded from good to bad, depending on the function it served. Likewise neutral events become good or bad only after we direct our attention on them. A rain in dry season is good, when causing flooding—bad. Yet the seasonal flooding in African plains assures survival of many species. Likewise even slight drizzle during a celebratory parade is regarded with dismay. We associate (judge) a forest fire with destruction, yet it serves as a necessary rejuvenation of the habitat.

And so on.

Until the moment of judgment, all is suspended in virtual existence. We might call is the kingdom of heaven, primordial chaos, Eden, paradise, or whatever precedes the manifestation in a dualistic reality. No wonder so few people can penetrate the mysteries of Quantum Theory as it seems to define comparable attributes. In some cases it even states that the act of measurement, the passing of judgment, defines its properties.[3]

The art of returning to Eden is to suspend the function of subjective judgment. We can only do so by bypassing information stored in our subconscious. If we succeed, we find ourselves in Eden where all things are potentially whatever we want them to be. They are not (yet) in a state of becoming but *are*; they do not affect but have the potential to do so. They are suspended in the eternal now, for there is no limit on the time when they can leave their virtual existence and cross the isthmus to the realm of becoming. And they then, and only then, become good or bad. We, humans, define their characteristics.[4]

No one else.

We can learn techniques to avoid passing judgment. If we accept each other the way we are, and choose to expect a predisposition towards good (without defining what 'good' is), we shall be halfway there. Likewise if we walk Buddha's middle path, with constant inclination towards helping, aiding, sharing, regardless who asks us for help, a similar reality will unfold. If we lose the distinction between *us* and *them*, it will be easy. This trait, or ability, has been defined as loving one another.

The direct effect of the power of the non-judgment can be readily seen under hypnosis. When the influence of the subconscious is taken out of the equation, anyone can be persuaded to overcome seemingly excruciating pain, one can perform surgical operations without anaesthetic, with the patient perfectly relaxed. The reason is that under such conditions the patient is unable to pass comparative judgment over events taking place in or about his or her body.

There is a little secret I wish to share with you.

None of us have ever left Eden. It is always around us. It surrounds us on all sides. We just forgot what Eden is like. The art of living is not to remain in Eden, but to go in and out of this elusive consciousness at will.

***

001201

FOOTNOTES

(1). Genesis 3:22. This reference appears modified later in John 5:22 in the statement "For the Father judges no man". The Father being in 'heaven', has no part in the duality of our realm. The "Lord God" of the Genesis refers to the I AM, the indwelling Christ, or the High Self, which was not as yet fully incorporate.

(2). Fright is an instinctive reaction, which mobilizes adrenaline to zero in on built-in defenses.

(3). For the aficionados of physics, I am referring to the Heisenberg uncertainty principle which states that our simultaneous knowledge of the location and motion of a particle is limited. The more we know about one property, the less we know about the other.

(4). It is amazing that this scientific knowledge has been known to man for thousands of years. Compare "For the Father judges no man, but hath committed all judgment unto the Son," John 5:22. The quote would be better understood if some translator or aspiring theologian hadn't decided to capitalize the letter S.

But the Kingdom is within you and it is without you.

Gospel of Thomas
(part) logion 3
Kapuscinski, Stanislaw *KEY TO IMMORTALITY*
[Inhousepress, Montreal 2001, Amazon Kindle & Kindle Editions 2010]

16

BE YE PERFECT

No way!

At first sight, this phrase sounds like a command to arrive at a dead end. After all, once we reach perfection what else is there? Even Mary Poppins stopped short. One cannot improve on perfection. Thus the command advocates total stagnation *ad infinitum*. That's a long time to be bored. Something doesn't sound right.

The above suggestion, command if you will, has been promulgated as part of the Sermon on the Mount. Even in the context of the Sermon, the postulate sounds peculiar. I checked the original Greek. Someone took liberties with the translation. In Greek, the word *teleios* means 'complete', rather than 'perfect'. 'Complete' also means 'whole', from which the word 'holy' is derived. Thus what the Teacher really said was Be ye Whole.

He told us to become complete.

Now here, on earth, we live in a state of consciousness which is split into spirit and matter, into good and evil, into duality. What Jesus had evidently advocated was that we must find the means to reconcile the duality within us. The duality of our consciousness. We are told that if we forget good and evil, black and white, left and right, and discover the source from which both states of consciousness emerge—we shall be better off. Whenever we see imperfection, we see absence of God. When we allow ourselves to pass judgment that differentiates between good and bad, we lose the unifying spirit, which is the very essence of our *true* nature. Since all things, actions, events, originate from the same source—all things are intrinsically good. Or at the very least, they are *for* our good. The first chapter of Genesis assures us of this. And if some things do not *seem* as good as others, well, at least we know, that they will pass. Everything on earth is transitory, ephemeral. *Sic transit gloria mundi.* So, why pay such attention to the transiency of matter? I am often amazed why do we pretend to ascribe to the Judeo-Christian ethic and then continue to ignore the very foundations on which it has been built.

Could it be just abject ignorance?

Over the last three-score years, I met two people who actually read the whole Bible. I heard of others, but I met just two. One insisted on literal interpretation of the events described therein, the other insisted that the Bible is 10% spiritual teaching, and the rest a historical account of Jewish people.

In my view, both of my dear friends are mistaken.

Now I have no intention to impose my own interpretation on anyone. What I do wish to share with you is a thought, that if, IF, we take either of my friends' point of view, we shall arrive at countless accounts which contradict our scientific knowledge, or we'll end up with a collection of mysteries which so many churches or religions specialize in. If, on the other hand, we chose to treat the Scriptures as reference textbooks which, when followed, will enhance our lives, lead us from mystery to enlightenment, from suffering to rejoicing, from poverty to a bountiful life, then we shall need to make an intense effort to understand the sublime teaching hidden within their pages.

Why hidden?

To protect the teaching. Knowledge means power, and power is abused by all who gain it prematurely. In spite of shrouding the wisdom in coats of parables, symbolism and historical allegories, three of the world's great religions managed to twist the teaching almost beyond recognition. The case in point is the title of today's essay. How can anyone wish to be perfect? Even if it were possible? Surely, all that we would have left to do would be to curl up and die. There would be nothing else for us to do.

Perfection is ever a *virtual* state, never one manifested in the visible world.

If, on the other hand, the meaning of the commandment is as I suggest, then the arrival at 'wholeness', thus being 'complete' marks the *beginning* of life. True life, not half witted, ignorant life of fear, doubt and perplexing mystery.

No Scriptures were ever written to become excuses for the creation of organized religions. The ancient writings secrete knowledge accumulated over millennia of human development. They have been written not by 'priests' in today's sense of the word, but by guardians of knowledge pertaining to the wisdom of life. And to partake in the fullness of life, we must first become complete. We must reunite our physical and spiritual nature. Heaven, as most of us know, is not a place reserved for the kindly old ladies baking cookies for needy children (though I tasted their cookies and I enjoyed them very much), but it represents a state of consciousness in which nothing, *nothing*, is impossible. The millions of 'miracles' manifested over thousands of years, attest loudly to this thesis. Each day new 'miracles' are invented. Heaven is a state of consciousness that dwells deep within us, and the Scriptures offer us countless examples how to discover it. If we do not understand those lessons, then we do not understand the Bible—or any of the Scriptures adopted (one could say usurped) by any religion. Perhaps it is time we should ask the priesthood to return our Book to us. Our need seems greater then theirs. After all, until we reconcile our duality, we shall remain half-finished, perhaps half-baked, and worse still... half-witted.

So, if I may suggest, do not try to be perfect, but do try hard to become whole. Complete. Start with the first step. Then the second, then... It is by far the most noble, fascinating, enchanting, and intriguing journey you will ever make.

It's up to you.

***

001202

The knower and the known are one.
Simple people imagine that they should see God
as if he stood there and they here.
This is not so.
God and I, we are one in knowledge.

Meister Eckhart
(c.1260—c.1328)

17

THE CHICKEN AND THE EGG

What is more likely?
Is it more likely that billions upon billions of stars have been born, by accident, out of nothing, and after manifesting their presence in the universe for many billions of years, in the fullness of their time, they entered a period of gradual collapse, lingering for aeons in protracted deaths, in the throes of which, quite accidentally, heavier atomic structures formed which would, eventually, constitute indispensable building blocks of biological life. And to deliver these building blocks into regions propitious for further development, the stars, quite accidentally, through cataclysmic supernovae explosions, crossed light-years of empty space to elsewhere and elsewhen.....

All quite accidentally.

And in the fullness of their time the gaseous star-clouds of rarefied matter congealed, accidentally, into new generations of stars, of planets, now endowed with not just hydrogen and helium but other heavy atoms necessary to create, eventually, complex chemical compounds.....

And while some particles created in the hearts of dying stars far away in the vastness of space would provide the necessary material for the ultimate creation of the oceans, and atmospheres and carbon compounds... other senseless atoms arranged themselves, quite accidentally yet in strict conformity to quite accidental laws of the universe, into incredibly complex relationships which, for no apparent reason, reproduced themselves into ever more complex molecules, until, quite accidentally they came into confluence of such accidental unions as to result in, what we now call, intelligence...

...which, after further countless millennia, began to manifest themselves as *intangible, ineffable, impalpable units of consciousness*?

This is a quasi-scientific fable. A fable based on the observation of the past.

Is there another way?

Is it more likely that an *Intangible, Ineffable, Impalpable Consciousness* directed Its attention upon Its own inexhaustible virtual potential thus bringing into manifestation energy which, in the fullness of time, due to its inherent predisposition, transmuted itself into an impalpable, intangible, effervescent Universal Presence. Then, this very same *Ineffable Consciousness* responding once more to Its nature, manifested Its inherent predisposition into Universal Laws which acted upon the effervescent emanations of Itself, until these emanations stirred with angular momentum to congeal, slowly, ever so slowly, into countless billions upon billions of stars....

Stars which, after further billions of years, in response to the Universal Laws, condensed into the prescribed atomic structures. These primitive nuclei, after yet further aeons and in strict conformity with the stringent, infallible Laws, increased their complexity by joining into molecules, that ultimately resulted in amino-acids, which, after yet further aeons of evolution...

After aeons of trials and errors....

Ever improving, experimenting, always in response to Its Primary Predisposition, resulted in a model which resembled

THE CHICKEN AND THE EGG

the structure of the principle manifested in the universe Itself, on a micro scale, and which model, after many more fragments of eternity, came to manifest the rudimentary characteristics of intelligence.

And then, after but a short fragment of eternity, the rudimentary model endowed with intelligence, almost suddenly, as if by a miracle, began to detect within itself a Presence, a mysterious yet wonderful, powerful yet benevolent, mystic, inexplicable yet so very close, *Intangible, Ineffable, Impalpable Consciousness.*

Which was first, the cosmic chicken or the cosmic egg?

Do we start with the results and wonder how those results came to be? That's exactly what science is all about. The scientists start with the end, with light which left a distant star millions of years ago, and they study it's spectrum to learn what might be it's structure, or rather, what the structure of the star might have been millions of years ago. For all the scientists know, they are studying what is no longer there. They act like galactic pathologists—studying the dead and the dying. The star might have turned into a red dwarf, might have collapsed into a neutron star, or even completely disappeared into the impenetrable enigma of a black hole. But the star is so many light-years away that we might not know any of this for further millions of years.

Others, the down-to-earth scientists, do hardly better. In the vast field of applied sciences, they study pathological conditions of plants, animals and humans, they invent semi-intelligible words to describe their findings, and then proceed to invent poisons to overcome the symptoms that their findings declared. We all do it. We all learn from our mistakes. Sometimes it seems that there is no other way.

But there is.

Even the scientists might, perhaps, in the fullness of their time, stop wondering about the distant past and look at the Present. And then they might notice, even as Carl Sagan did, eventually, that *We live in a universe remarkably hospitable to life.*[1]

Remarkably hospitable.....

This remarkable blessing has been always known to the mystics, the prophets, and to the artists. They recognized early on that life is not a biological infestation, but that our biological structures are but a means, a channel designed to partake in the eternal function of creation. Prophets are said to see the future, even as artists do. The artists see that which has not yet happened, which is yet to be.

The real artists, the painters, sculptors, composers, poets do not look for past errors. They start with the Source. They start with the premise that all creation is inspired by the *Intangible, the Ineffable, the Impalpable*. They discard their early mistakes, destroy or ignore them, and strive to do better. Always better. They strive to attune themselves with That which inspires them. They strive to become channels for Creative Life Force Itself prodigious at the core of their being. They endeavor to lose themselves, to lose their insignificance, by blending with the Whole.

And they grow rich in their rewards. Not in terms of the silver and gold which define success for the often well meaning, often semi-literate professional athletes, rock "musicians", legalized bootleggers and so many others whose sole purpose in life is the pursuit of Mammon.[2] The artists' wealth is counted neither in gold nor in the mighty dollar.

Their riches amass within. They exfoliate without.

When they reach for the stars, they are untouched by the furtive rays of the dying giants. They bask in the shimmering light streaming directly into their hearts from ever the same inexhaustible Source.

From the *Intangible, Ineffable, Impalpable, Eternal Consciousness.*

***

FOOTNOTES

(1). Sagan, Carl THE COSMIC CONNECTION produced by Jerome Agel [Dell Publishing Co., Inc. New York, 1973] pg. 257.

(2). While I have no recent data on the rock 'musicians', The Associated Press published baseball players salaries ranging from $12,500,000 to $25,200,000 per year. The last is a contract for 10 years amounting to $252,000,000. Potential incentive bonuses are extra. [Gleamed from THE GAZETTE, Montreal, Dec.12, 2000]

Imaginary time may sound like science fiction, but it is in fact a well-defined mathematical concept.

...for the purposes of the calculation one must measure time using imaginary numbers, rather than real ones. This has an interesting effect on space-time: the distinction between time and space disappears completely.

Stephen Hawking
A BRIEF HISTORY OF TIME
[Bantam Books, Toronto 1988; pg.134].
Refer also to a more extensive discussion of the concept of time in Kapuscinski's
VISUALIZATION—CREATING YOUR OWN UNIVERSE,
chapter on *Aging and Longevity*.
[Inhousepress, Montreal, 2001 & Amazon Kindle 2010]

18

THE CHURCH

Sometime ago a dear friend of mine, having read some of my essays, suggested that, on occasion, he had an impression that I have it 'in' for the Church. He was very polite about it, but, "Well," he said, "you don't seem to find much good to say about the Holy Mother the Church."
What could I say? I don't.
Not much.
Not for as long as the Church, the Holy Roman Catholic and Apostolic Church takes it upon herself to speak on matters pertaining to the teaching of Christ. For try as I would, each time I attempted to reconcile Christ's teaching with the Church's manifest philosophy, I have been reminded of a man who asked: *"Master, what good thing shall I do, that I may have eternal life?"* And after a preliminary discussion the answer came loud and clear: *"...go and sell that thou hast, and give to the poor, and thou shall have treasure in heaven: and come and follow me."*[1] The last 2000 years made it abundantly clear that the Church has absolutely no interest in any treasures in heaven. On the other hand, the brazen agglomeration of priceless wealth which I suspect exceeds even that of the British Empire which R. Buckminster Fuller once called: "...history's most successful world-outlaw organization..." leaves me full of admiration.[2] However, since the Church wouldn't follow the Christ, I could hardly be expected to follow the Church.
But this is true *only* of the area of my particular interest. The area of inquiry into the nature of being. A personal inquiry into the legacy of past Masters which, to this day,

appears to remain obscure, enigmatic, full of mystery, to all but few members of the Holy Mother I've ever met.

Perhaps I should meet more people.

On the other hand, I have nothing but admiration and undying gratitude to the Church, present and past, in many other areas that are *almost* as dear to me. I wish my readers, and particularly my friend, to know that I hold the Church responsible for my countless moments of joy, of visual, aural and tactile pleasure that contribute greatly to the fabric of my daily life. In fact, outside my marriage, no other organization contributed so abundantly to the pleasure of my senses as the Church.

Let me count the ways.

I held my breath as I entered the Basilica of Saint Peter. What magnificent space, what resplendent vistas! I dare anyone, of any faith or religion, not to derive pleasure, not to admire the euphoric splendor (spiritual decadence only if you are a spoilsport) of the central building of the Church. The sensuously polished marbles, the forests of columns— forthright and upright, soaring towards heavenly domes or multihued and spiral, mysterious. The armies of sculptured saints, the galleries of paintings of more saintly figures, all immortalized right here, on earth, for posterity. The greatest names of the 16th century, Bramante, Michelangelo and Raphael have been mustered to contribute their genius to this monument of human endeavor. And all this thanks to but one man, Pope Julius II. Admittedly there are those who call his reign "the decadence of papacy,"[3] but there is another way of looking at this period. Without Julius, St. Peter would never have happened.

And then there is the Sistine Chapel ceiling, the papal apartments, the papal portrait galleries, the inexhaustible works of art in the Vatican Museum, the consummate splendor of other Vatican buildings, the gardens... and, last but not least, the superb archives of the Vatican library...

Who else could provide us with such unprecedented riches?

And this is just the headquarters.

Wherever I went, wherever I have traveled, in Europe, in Africa, in North, Central or South America, everywhere, in every country, my joy was multiplied by the sheer numbers of beautiful churches, often amassing the best art and architecture that money could buy of local and imported talent. Often of genius left unknown, forgotten in small Brazilian, Mexican, Peruvian towns, in neglected English villages, in small hamlets the world over. The Gothic style alone could not have been inspired by any authority other than the Church. The Early English, the Decorated, the Curvilinear or Flamboyant, the sedate more reserved Tudor, all testify to the Church reaching ever higher, ever more lugubriously, for something she seems to have lost. But for me, for my own pleasure, the heritage speaks of nothing but beauty, of human endeavor, of the creative spirit.

And then, by unmitigated contrast I saw the inspiring, flowing, soaring effects of Amiens and other ecclesiastic monuments of the great French Cathedral cities... High towers, pinnacles, superabundant sculpture, effervescent stained glass filtering preternatural light to the streamlined interiors. Wherever the Church stretched her mighty arms, she left an indelible mark of beauty in her prodigious wake.

And then there is music.

I defy anyone to point to any other source as abundant as the Church in commanding composers to produce their best for the good of all. Music cannot be retained by those who commissioned its fervor. It is a free gift to all that would listen. From the *aria antiqua*, through the doleful canticles to the Ambrosian and Gregorian chants echoing among the stone walls of ancient monasteries, to Handel's Messiah and other Oratorios. And who could claim that Bach wasn't first and foremost a church's composer? And then we find Tosca's incomparable *Vissi d'arte*, Desdemona's plaintive *Ave Maria*, Elizabeth de Valois's *Tu che le vanita conoscesti* and so many other sublime arias all, surely, inspired by the Church's teaching. And finally there is Mozart who, through his ecstatic prodigious and ebullient *Requiem* allowed us a peak into his personal heaven. Could any of these have been born without the Church's influence?

I think not.

And there is more—much more...

So I am to this day, and intend to remain, grateful to the Church, to the Holy Mother. Grateful for her past inspiration and for giving access to us all, today, to share in her splendid, unequal aegis. And to those who belittle her wealth, I can only ask: Who else is prepared to spend millions, countless millions, on the maintenance of such legacy?

Perhaps this fact alone is the greatest blessing. The Church is assuring that the wonder of human creativity will remain accessible not only to us but also to our children's children. Who says the Church cannot serve two masters? Perhaps we should forgive and forget the preacher's peccadilloes and be grateful for his obvious achievements. By standing on guard of such illustrious past, perhaps the Church might also inspire our distant future.

And, after all, the future is our own.

***

001207

FOOTNOTES

(1). Matthew 19:16-21
(2). Fuller, R. Buckminster, CRITICAL PATH [St. Martin's press, New York 1981;pg. 58]
(3). Kenneth Clark CIVILIZATION [British Broadcasting Corp. 1969] pg. 118.

19

MIRROR OF A LESSER GOD

In my earlier essay entitled *Mirror*[1], I quoted a phrase from the Apocryphal Acts of John: *A lamp am I to you that perceive me—A mirror am I to you that know me.* The *Mirror* refers, of course, to the divine spark within us which in the initial stages of our spiritual unfoldment acts as a guide, later, when we grow more cognizant of our true nature, It becomes a Mirror of our true Self. Some months after I wrote that essay, I recall seeing a film (a movie) called "Children of a Lesser God." Right then it struck me that long before we become aware of the divinity within us, most of us can take advantage of a similar reflection in what I thought of as a "Mirror of a Lesser God." Without any implicit or explicit connotations, in this context the "lesser god" is, or could be, our own mate. Our husband or wife. It seemed to me that in marriage, we act as mirrors to each other.

Or should be.

No one ever told me that they were fully aware of their (obvious) faults, but thought them so minor as not to warrant any remedial measures. Our nature, however, has disposed us to be aware of our own shortcomings only when exemplified in another person. This predisposition to see our own weaknesses in others, particularly one as close to us as our mate, is tempered by, what we call, love. We see the apparent or imagined foibles in our beloved but, due to our emotional commitment (in this case matrimonial bond), we endeavor to rise above them. We see that he or she does not live up to our standards, but we 'forgive' them. We are seldom, if ever, aware that we discern almost exclusively our own weaknesses reflected in the personified mirror we have chosen to spend our life with.

At first this may sound absurd.

How can anyone as perfect as myself have so many faults? After all, when we first met he (she) didn't have any of these so very obvious imperfections. Surely, he (she) was a veritable Mary Poppins. Virile (sweet), handsome (beautiful), understanding, forgiving, willing to do anything I asked. Never tired, always full of energy. If I were him (her), I'd do something to act (be) younger.[2]

But these are trite examples.

The important thing is that if we do accept our mates as mirrors of our character, we can learn a great deal about ourselves. We can see what is wrong with us, *without* telling anyone about it. We can take full advantage of our 'mirror', without ever sharing our knowledge even with our mate. Not even in secret. Whatever blemishes, whatever imperfections we see, big or small, *they are our own*. Our own, personal mirror is a window into our own soul. Perhaps, just as well...

If I see messiness—I'm messy. If I see laziness—I'm lazy. If I see my mate overeating—chances are I'm getting fat. If I think she (he) is stupid—I have a lot to learn. If I expect more respect—I don't give enough respect to others. If she (he) is short-tempered (in my eyes)—I need more self-control. If I see her (him) failing in her (his) duties—I need to review my own responsibilities.

There is no end of examples.

Have you noticed how, husband and wife, over the years, seem to grow more and more alike? By judging each other we attract each other's characteristics to ourselves. Like attracts like. This is part of karma.

Like everything else on earth, mirrors are relative. Sometimes the mirror has some scratches, seems a little dusty, and doesn't offer the very best reflection. Sometimes we need corrective lenses before we can spot the truth in the reflection. But more often than not the problem lies not in our eyes but in the way we use them. We can study our mirrors visually, but also with our other senses. Also with our emotions, even our mind.

Perfection cannot behold evil.

A perfect man would only see the True Self of another person, the Divine Spark if you will, and thus not be aware of any imperfection. To see shortcomings we must pass judgment and reaction. But, if we really want to, we can refuse to play the game. We can rise above it. this act alone makes us less than perfect. And, after all, each time we judge another, we extract judgment from them—often with accumulated interest. Reality is like that. It is a case of action and

For as long as we find fault with one another, we remain children of a lesser god, the god of ego. Our mirrors, while also imperfect, are nevertheless entities of divine potential. For this reason alone we must treat them with the greatest respect. After all, when we suspend all judgment, we shall no longer detect any weakness in our reflections. You or I shall see, and become, as John might have said in his Apocryphal Acts, *A perfect mirror to him and her who know me.*

[Kiciuni, Xmas 2000]

***

001225

FOOTNOTES

(1). BEYOND RELIGION Vol. II, March 1999 [Inhousepress, Montreal 2000, Paperback 2015]

(2). For the uninitiated, Mary Poppins is an imaginary character who calls herself "almost perfect."

Beautiful faces are those that wear –
It matters little if dark or fair—
Whole-souled honesty printed there.

Beautiful eye are those that show,
Like crystal panes where hearthfires glow,
Beautiful thoughts that burn below.

***

Beautiful lives are those that bless
Silent rivers of happiness,
Whose hidden fountains but few may guess.

Ellen P. Allerton
Excerpt from a poem *Beautiful Things*, from a collection by Hazel Felleman:
THE BEST LOVED POEMS OF THE AMERICAN PEOPLE
[Garden City Books, New York, 1936]

20

ETERNAL DAMNATION

Few concepts are as wonderful as Eternal Damnation! I can now hear even my best friends saying: "Now, finally, our author's gone mad. Berserk. He simply lost his senses."
Perhaps, but... don't count on it.
Not just yet.

There is a strange statement in the Revelation of John. It purports quite simply: *"Behold, I make all things new."*[1] John does not appear to imply that all things *old* cease to exist, but rather that all the things which form part and parcel of our reality, by some strange twist of fate, *become* new. Fresh. Different. Whatever was black, seems to be turning white. Whatever was ugly now shows a tendency towards beauty. Whatever was evil, now loses its demonic flavor. Whatever once caused sadness, now, as though by magic, seems to lead to joy. All things, all events, all people are seen in strangely different light. In a new, lustrous light.
For instance.
Sickness is 'evil', but not if it forestalls a greater misery. A man developing a cough may suffer enough to stop smoking, *before* he plummets into the bane of cancer. He may stop short just in time. Thanks to his propitious sickness.
And if he doesn't stop smoking and does succumb to cancerous lungs, well, the sickness will curtail his life in this particular body, which he abused beyond its capacity to give

him pleasure. He dies, 're-programs' his concept of living, and enters another body to try and try again. Evidence of infinite mercy. Of unlimited love.

Behold, I make all things new...

Ability to see good in everything is not a neurotic bent, but the singular means, an unrivalled method to find joy in *all* aspects of one's life. This ability, and this ability alone, assures us of abiding in heaven, which, as has been discussed in many of my essays, is a curious and inimitable state of consciousness. A time will come when men, women, will shed at will their physical bodies, spend fragments of eternity in the Ocean of Infinite Potential, and return refreshed to experiment with new, hitherto untried adventures. This is what is meant by being in but not of this world. By being the observer and the observed at the same time. In a way, we are already doing just that through the miracle of reincarnation, but later, in years to come, we shall do so on a daily basis, even as the great Masters of the past have done it, and as Sai Baba appears to do daily, perhaps any instant, at will, at his bidding, in moments of need or daring.

So what of damnation? Eternal Damnation?

It is an eternal blessing—not, of course, the old, religious concept of eternal suffering. Only a twisted mind can create a God who would sanction integral parts of Himself to suffer for an instant, let alone forever. In higher reality all suffering is imaginary, at worst, transient, ephemeral. The concept is only there to serve us. Our true being is beyond suffering, beyond the touch of evil, of religious dichotomy. Whatever Source we recognize as God, this Source is Omnipresent, synonymous with Goodness, with Love, Life, Intelligence, and all the attributes necessary for the Act of Becoming in joy and fulfillment. When all things become new, we become aware of it.

So what of... Damnation?

We are, essentially, three beings in one. We are our body, our mind and we are also spirit. Spirit is incorruptible by deed, time or becoming. The body is transient, little more than an out-picturing of our mental processes. It is the mind that is the sole creator of our reality. Yet while mind and body intermingle, we seem to attach our awareness to this construct or amalgam. In a way, our body illustrates how we see ourselves, our mind—as others see us.[2] But our body is also the product of not only the universal mind which provides all the building blocks necessary to produce a physical construct, but of a matrix of instructions, of blueprints—as it were—which are a directs result of our subconscious, that in turn houses knowledge accumulated over millions of years of evolution.

Now, whenever we experience a new vision of Truth, this new image, though fragmentary, is worth saving. Truth, as we all know, is one, but there are as many forms of Its conscious expression as there are living entities in the universe. But all nonsense, such as belief in suffering, such as the devil, or Satan, or the reality of evil, is destined for Eternal Damnation. Each time we start again, in a new body, such concepts are destroyed forever. They die with our physical bodies. Have you noticed the unadulterated innocence in newborn baby's eyes? There is no evil there, nor a shadow of evil, no negative remnants from his or her previous life. All harmful miscreant concepts have been destroyed forever. Condemned. They've been burned in eternal fire. They have not been worth saving.[3]

And thus, thanks to Eternal Damnation, through the intricacies of Divine Wisdom, we are not born, nor reborn, with a concept of evil. We start again as pure and innocent manifestations of the Whole, with the Eternal Spark ever our Guardian.[4] And one day, one wonderful day, we become aware of this enigmatic Presence.

On that day, as if by magic, all things become new.

On that momentous day we take our first tentative step towards the infinity of heaven. We no longer need the blessing of Eternal Damnation to rid us of wrong concepts, of misleading illusions. In fact, we have taken our first step towards Eternal Life.

And we never look back.

***
001209

FOOTNOTES

(1). Revelation of Saint John the Divine 21:5

(2). In a discourse delivered on November 19,1999, Sai Baba put it this way: "You are not one person but three—the one you think you are (physical body), the one others think you are (mental body), and the one you really are (the principle of Atma)."

(3). Anyone interested in this matter can read further on the subject in *Salvation* (April 1997) and *Sanctifying* (March 1997), BEYOND RELIGION, Collected Essays Vol. I. [Inhousepress Montreal 1999, 2001, Amazon Kindle Edition 2010]

(4). Admittedly we do carry our karma from previous lives, but we are given an unbiased chance to nullify it without preconceived negative ideas.

For now we see through a glass, darkly; but then face to face: now I know in part; but then shall I know even as also I am known.

Paul the Apostle, Corinthians I, 13:12

21

ECUMENISM

Faith is what draws us together, religion—what sets us apart.

The reason is very simple. Should the Churches grant their members the (God given) free will, they would automatically lose their *raison d'être*. The Churches, not the people. A religion is a system of controlling people, to the same degree as any other organization that expects its members to conform to a single set of rules. Whether we deem such rules 'good' or 'bad', whether we call them a constitution or a *credo* is coincidental. As you apply for a citizenship of a country or a membership of a church, you must forfeit a portion of your personal freedom and accept all the imposed regimes, laws, rules and regulations or commandments.

Obey or get out—or at least go to jail.

All nations lay claim to having the best system of government for their people. They so *claim*. The same is true of the churches. I've never heard of a church, a religion, which asserted that their system, their teaching, is inferior to another, but... let's do it anyway. No! The reason why the churches are orthodox is that they all think that they are right. Infallibly right.

Right? Look around.

Whether we examine long established religions, or the New Age regimes popping up like mushrooms after a summer shower, the method is invariably the same. Obey me or go to hell or jail—depending on the organization. Sometimes both.

Let us take a cursory look at some diverse faiths. I say 'diverse' because we tend to think that they are different. If fact, faith has little-to-nothing to do with religions. Faith is that, within us, which *knows*, which is so deeply rooted in our unconscious, that even the most oppressive religious fanatics seldom manage to suppress it. Faith originates with the divine within, religion with the mundane without.

Some years ago, I've written an essay on *Power*.[1] In it, I proposed that Power, through compromise, lead to corruption. (The end product is not an original conclusion). I seem to have come a full circle. It is evident that religions (as do their secular counterparts) invariably require compromise. No ecumenism is possible without it. Yet, strange though it may seem, faith needs no such dilution. It stands supreme, untouched by compromise, by diminution. Let us glance, but briefly, at just one maxim coming to us in so many ways but from a single Source.

We are all conversant with Buddha's central philosophical theme that we should all travel the Middle Path. Buddha experimented with both extremes, with exorbitant riches and dire poverty, and, ultimately, found Truth in the middle. A path which rejects *all* extremes. It corresponds in Christianity to the road that is straight and narrow; one from which it is extremely easy to fall off in a (religious) reality which is firmly anchored to the principle of duality. Likewise I strongly suspect that only in the middle we can find "peace... which passeth all understanding."[2]

Bhagavad-Gita, the Hindu scripture that epitomizes the ancient science of the Vedic literature, states quite succinctly: He *who is without affection either for good or evil is firmly fixed in perfect knowledge.*[3] "Neither good nor evil" sounds very much like the middle ground. And later: There *is no possibility of one's becoming a yogi, O Arjuna, if one eats too*

much or eats too little, sleeps too much or does not sleep enough.[4]
That simple.

The Christian creed echoes this sentiment in the statement that "*...narrow is the way, which leadeth unto life,*"[5] and further admonishes us to suspend all judgment.[6] We must conclude that by suspending all judgment we shall revert to the Middle Ground that is to the Straight and Narrow Path.

Regrettably the Jewish as well as the Christian religions are steeped so deeply in duality that it's not easy to find a middle ground strong enough to sustain an ecumenical union. Both religions affirm that God is one, but then proceed to flounder in reprimands pertaining to evil, devil, hell and other dualistic concepts that they endow with unprecedented power. Little or no effort has been made by the biblical scribes to stress the illusory character of 'evil', and that dualism is, *per se*, the product of our judgmental nature rather than of Objective Reality.

I strongly suspect that the dilution of the original Truth, at least among Christians, is principally the result of three factors:

1. The elimination of Gnostic philosophy from the orthodox teaching; (I am of the opinion that Gnostic philosophy had been never understood by the religious administrators of the day);[7]

2. The time which elapsed between the original teaching and its recording in a written form;

3. The attempts by many scribes to 'improve' on the original texts in the countless manual (and later mechanical) re-writes of the various, all too numerous and fragmented scriptures.

We find echoes of what might have been in such statements as "resist not evil" or in Jesus' oft-repeated lament: "How is it that ye do not understand?"[8]—but these are seldom given prominence in the orthodox teaching. Perhaps the Truth is buried somewhere deep in the Vatican archives to which we, wandering pilgrims, have no access.

Regrettably, until and unless the Judeo-Christian ethic rejects the reality of evil, there is little chance of an ecumenical success. The leaders of orthodoxy will remain stubborn in their righteousness, as dualistic religions must be. Perhaps they forget that, to quote Bhaktivedanta: *"Religion without philosophy is sentiment, or sometimes fanaticism, while philosophy without religion is mental speculation.*[9]

The mind and spirit must be aligned in the same direction.

The same can be said of Islam in its many expressions, of Zoroastrianism, and many other less populous religions espousing dualism.

But all is not lost.

It is apparent that most religions advocate faith in One God. What differs is the method of achieving awareness of this Single Deity. One day churches will grasp that every human being must arrive at his or her individual realization of the Divine. On that day there will be a single church and a single religion based on faith and not on sacerdotal need to control people. On that day we shall all heed Sai Baba's words:

There is only one religion, the religion of love.

From time to time, we are blessed with mystics who, even if for a short while, keep the flame of Truth burning. Perhaps the time is ripe for more such men to make their mark on our meandering journey. I leave you with the words of one such spiritual giant given us by the Sufis (a by-product of Islam), Jalal-ud-Din Rumi. Rumi's depth of perception shines in his inspired invitation that I shall quote, hopefully accurately, from memory: *"Beyond the ideas of doing right and doing wrong there is a field. I'll meet you there."* You too are invited.

***

001212

FOOTNOTES

(1). Philippians 4:7.
(2). Chapter II, text 57. BHAGAVAD-GITA AS IT IS, translations and purports by His Divine Grace A.C. Bhaktivedanta Swami Prabhupada [The Bhadtivedanta Book Trust, Los Angeles 1968,1972]
(3). ibid., Chapter 6, text 16. Yogi, in this context, means a man who reached perfect knowledge.
(4). Matth. 7:14
(5). "Judge not." Luke 6:37, Matth. 7:1.
(6). The text of Shema: "Hear O Israel: the Lord our God is one Lord" Deut. 6:4, Mark 12:29
(7). I refer to Gnosticism in the broadest possible terms. I think of it as that knowledge which one actually lives by. It is knowledge derived from within not from without. It is your own knowledge, not imposed by somebody else.
(8). Mark 8:21 et al.
(9). BHAGAVAD-GITA, ibid., purport page 45.

*Fishes, asking what water was, went to a wise fish.
He told them that it was all around them,
yet they still thought that they were thirsty.*

Nasafi

22

CONSCIOUSNESS

A term so simple yet so twisted by medical, philosophical, psychiatric and religious jargon as to render it into the realm of mystery, fanaticism, often of utter nonsense. Consciousness, quite simply, is a synonym for individualized Soul. It is the way the Universal Consciousness manifests as life. Even as our physical bodies objectify and demonstrate biological life through trillions of individual interconnected cells, so Soul does likewise through countless units of awareness. While various religions have laid claim to monopoly over the administration of our 'souls', no one, no religious authority, has yet usurped control over our consciousness. Not officially.

Not in so many words...

Yet, through the long litanies of commandments, laws, dogmas, instructions, threats and rewards, and countless other imposed regimes, the various governments, churches and other 'authorities' do try to modulate our consciousness. They have to. Should they stop, they'd lose their *raison d'être*. For them control is like blood to a biological entity. Take away their control and they whimper, shrink and collapse. Look at the many past empires: The ancient Egyptian, later the Roman, the recent British Empire, the Communist Oligarchy, the power wielded by Vatican during the Middle Ages. Now, finally, after thousands of years of mental and emotional imposition, "the king is dead." God save the king!

Today, you are the king. The new king.

The end is coming...

No, not the end of the world, but the end to man's ability to control the mind of another. The end will happen soon, at the onset of this Age of Aquarius, which we have now breached in full swing. Everything—every idea, invention, discovery—which empowers an *individual* is a manifestation of this New Era. During the next 2000 years people will learn to think for themselves. Many are still relying on others to tell them what to do, what to believe in, what is "right or wrong." For them it will not be easy but their *consciousness* will guide them.

Spurious attempts to dominate our thoughts will not deter us. Our consciousness does *not* consist of our thoughts. To use an expression from Bhagavad-Gita, consciousness is "*...that which pervades the entire body*".[1] Yet, if we destroy the body, the 'soul', or more accurately the *consciousness* remains unharmed. Consciousness is the nearest to what we can define as our True Being. It may inhabit a physical, emotional, mental or spiritual body. Usually all of them simultaneously. It 'uses' a body to 'live'. To experience, change. Progress.

A material body is its mode of being.

Needless to say, consciousness does not remain in a body that is no longer useful to it. As the body ceases to function, consciousness withdraws its presence, even as it does, to a degree, when not needed (although the body remains biologically active). Such moments of partial withdrawal take place during states of intense contemplation, during a particularly deep trance of hypnosis, occasionally during sleep, and even when our bodies are knocked out in a street accident or a boxing ring. The only difference is that in the examples listed our consciousness retains the ability to return to the body and raise it from its 'dormant' state. This link is known in esoteric circles as the silver cord, in more up-to-date language in can be detected in subtle brain activity, even while other vital signs are in a passive mode. Since there is ample evidence that consciousness can go in and out of our bodies, is seems logical to assume that that which has the ability to continue to exist outside our body, is not dependent on the body for its existence.

And thus we should endeavor to define life not in terms of a biological process, but as the presence of consciousness. Our medical professionals are straddling this position, defining the presence of consciousness as an impulse registering on the electroencephalograph. Even cardiac arrest no longer suffices to certify death. At present, the brain impulse is the final word. What the medical profession fails to realize is that even the weakest brain activity is the result of latent consciousness, not it's cause.

Yet the residual brain waves may be so subtle that our present day instruments might fail to detect them. There have been cases when no vital signs were detectable for many minutes, occasionally hours, yet the body revived.

The silver cord had not been severed.

As mentioned or implied in a number of my essays, we must learn not to treat various scriptures as religious dissertations but begin interpreting them as sources of scientific observations amassed over millennia of human history. In so doing, we would greatly benefit in our knowledge not how to die, but how to live.

We must also learn to stand back and observe our consciousness within our own being. We must learn to be the observer and the observed, simultaneously. In time, we shall learn that the two are One. To quote the commentator of the Bhagavad-Gita once more: One *can understand the nature of the Supreme by thorough study of oneself.*[(2)] Or as Jesus put it, *I and my Father are one.*[(3)]

So are you. You and your Consciousness are One. The same holds true for every single human being. And even

more, although you, or I, are but a fraction of the Whole, *qualitatively* you are One with the Whole, with God. Identical. There is but One Consciousness. And we are inexorably liked to It through the attribute known as the individualized Soul. As we learn of our true nature we discover our own, individual, immortality. There is no other way. And, what's more, "narrow is the way". We shall never find the Supreme, the Divine, in books. What we must do is to place our attention on It to the exclusion of everything else.
It is there, waiting.

***
001213

FOOTNOTES

(1). BHAVAGAD-GITA—AS IT IS, translations and purports by His Divine Grace A.C. Bhaktivedanta Swami Prabhupada [The Bhadtivedanta Book Trust, Los Angeles 1968,1972]
(2). ibid. pg. 26.
(3). John 10:30

When you are still fragmented, lacking certainty what difference does it make what your decisions are?

Hakim Sanai
[THE WALLED GARDEN OF TRUTH]

23

TRUTH

There are those among my readers who will accuse me of, on occasion, repeating similar themes. They will, of course, be right. The purpose of my essays is not to present a 'new' truth, but to attempt to expose and share the One and only Truth under many different names. The fact is that Truth, like Life and Love and all other attributes of the Infinite are, by definition, also infinite. And Truth, perhaps more than any other attribute, must be continually rediscovered, incorporated into new circumstances, allowed to influence new conditions, infused into seemingly innocuous fragments of life, shine light upon new problems, resolve new challenges.

There are basically only two types of people. The Bhagavad-Gita defines them as those possessed of transcendental nature, [Jesus' sons of the light][1] and those who exhibit demoniac qualities[2] whom Jesus called the sons of the devil, or just simply the dead.[3] The attributes of first lead to liberation, of the latter to bondage. But I am not really concerned here with the definition of the attributes at the metaphysical level. To me, the basis from which to start is the overview of reality.

The Big Picture.

We can start with the premise that matter, with its attendant and interchangeable energy, is the sole substance of the universe, or that there is also 'something' else, whatever it might be. This 'whatever' has stirred the mind of man ever since he came down from the protective branches of a tree, saw a diffused light of day probing the innards of a primordial cave, or took the first tentative steps on his hind legs. There is no time in history of man that he, our forefather, had not left evidence of some awareness of a Force, of 'something' besides material reality. In my essay on *Spirit*,[4] I illustrated the depth of this concept extant in the primitive tribes of central and South Africa. Where did such ideas come from? Which gene brought them to the attention of the ancients' frontal lobes? Or was it an indefinable affinity which caused the frontal lobe to become aware of it's motivational impulse.

An indefinable affinity.

I suggest that we all suffer from a festering, inherent need for at least some degree of logic in our lives. While moments of childish folly have their place, the vast majority of us suffer from an underlining current of hunger for order, harmony and beauty. It has been argued that even the primordial chaos exhibits these latent qualities, a predisposition towards order.[5] But if this is so, and today's solons of theoretical physics indicate that it is, then how did this predisposition find its way into chaos? If intelligence is the by-product of millions, even billions, of years of evolution, then why is there evidence that a predisposition toward order, harmony and beauty are extant in the primeval non-substance of chaos?

I defy anyone to answer this question.

Apparently, neither scientists nor philosophers can. To even speculate on the possible explanation we must assume *a priori* that the above mentioned predisposition existed *before* material manifestation, before the energy of a single atom congealed into a solid form, that intelligence which caused chaos to exhibit these qualities must have preceded the evolutionary spiral.

That it existed before the... Big Bang.[6]

It is this unknown factor that our forefathers named or defined as God. It was the ineffable Force, Being—if you prefer personification as Greeks did and Hindu still do—which (or who) predisposed matter, energy and the resultant evolutionary constructs toward the attributes inherent in the primordial reality, a reality preceding the subsequent creation of, what we now call, the universe.[7] In these terms, we can suggest a new definition of Truth. Truth is everything that is in accord with the intention of the Primordial Predisposition. If you are in unison with order, harmony and beauty, you are a manifestation of Truth. You *are* the Truth, if you conform to this definition to the letter. It seems that the three muses Beauty, Harmony and Order are waiting, latent, not only in the primordial chaos, but in the chaos of our minds, our ideas, concepts, in our puerile lack of understanding.

Eternally waiting, eternally available. Inexhaustible. Like a bottomless well.

It is hardly surprising that such realizations led our forefathers to enshroud their conclusions, if such they were, under the aegis of religion. At the time, the danger of casting pearls before swine was even more apt to be exploited than now. Imagine men, some two/three thousand years ago having the ability to crush an atom. Or place the H-bomb in the hands of Genghis Khan, Napoleon or Hitler. Even now, we only just managed to escape a nuclear winter. So far.

And let us make no mistake about it. As we learn to understand the universe, we learn to understand God. Or the manifested Truth. And such knowledge holds unprecedented power. Luckily, the scientists have not yet discovered the shortcut. But even then we are on the very brink of a revolutionary breakthrough.

The next momentous secret is ready to be discovered.

It lies in the knowledge held for us under the shroud of religious dogma. It is so simple that no man, certainly no priest of any worldly religion, dared to take it seriously. This secret motivated Einstein when he said "I want to know the thoughts of God, the rest are details." It is the secret of

Universal Unity. Yet, Einstein, in spite his genius, failed. He looked without instead of looking within. He had changed directions late in his life... By then, however, he had been too set in his ways. Let us not make the same mistake. We can discover the nature of God by studying the workings of the universe, but infinitely easier by studying the nature of man. We have been given a hint some 3500 years ago, when one man wrote that we are created onto the image and likeness of God. How come no one ever took this scientific statement seriously? No one but one man, the one who equated himself with the source of his being.

Today, the search is on. We have already started.

The next aspect of Truth we shall discover is that we, and the Sublime Essence, permeating the primordial chaos from which we have all emerged are one and the same. On that day, each one of us will stand up proudly, then bow in awe before the splendor of the greatest Truth of all, and say: I and my Father are one.

***

001214

FOOTNOTES

(1). John 12:36

(2). BHAGAVAD-GITA—AS IT IS, translations and purports by His Divine Grace A.C. Bhaktivedanta Swami Prabhupada [The Bhadtivedanta Book Trust, Los Angeles 1968,1972] Chapter 16, pg.236

(3). John 8:44 and Matth. 8:22 respectively

(4). BEYOND RELIGION Vol.II, *Spirit*, Sept.1997 [Inhousepress, Montreal 2000, Amazon Kindle Edition 2010]

(5). Hopefully, there are numerous books on Chaos Theory in your local library. If not I suggest you demand them! It is a fascinating subject.

(6). See essay on the CHICKEN AND THE EGG (hereinbefore)

(7). While for the sake of argument I use the past tense 'predisposed', creation is an ongoing process.

24

FREE WILL

The concept of free will is a conundrum for as long as we recognize that spirit is eternal whereas matter merely transient. This, of course, is not true. Even the advocates of the Big Bang theory do not preclude the possibility of a regenerating, or oscillating universe, a concept held for thousands of years by the wise men of the East.[1] The scientists hold that the universe having contracted (in the distant future) to a non-dimensional-non-space 'point' is, as likely as not, going to explode once again to form yet another universe in whose parameters, in the fullness of new time created in the process of the successive big-bang, intelligence will evolve once again.

Well... our scientists are partially right.

They usually are. The problem is that our theoretical-astrophysicists assisted by their cosmological, 'subnuclearly' inclined equally theoretical colleagues, continue to change their mind—rather often of late. They produce strings of theories, as well as theories of Strings, Super Strings, and end up all tied up in knots. As if there was only one way in which matter could be eternal.

Yet there is no need for such cataclysmic let alone catatonic origins. Matter spirals and is sucked into black holes all the time. There, it may well be transformed through countless mini-bangs into the necessary ingredients for the creation of new stars, new building blocks to house intelligences to come. It would, of course, be easier to accept any such theory if we were to assume that intelligence is there, waiting, in whatever form, to nudge the stardust in the right direction, and to be embodied, eventually, into the new constructs of the new biological or mechanical entities.

Alas, our scientists are not quite ready to be so logical. Not yet.

But why is it so necessary to assume the continuity of matter?

The reason is the philosophical assumption of Free Will. If matter, with its alter ego energy, were not eternal, then all those fragments of intelligence embodied in e.g. biological entities (that's you and me) which had not yet achieved *liberation* from the wheel of Awagawan (reincarnation), would be left high and dry. They would not be able to share the benefits of a world of matter in which to accelerate their evolution until such a time, as they would no longer require, to use a biblical expression, coats of skin.[2] God knows (no pun intended) that even in a dualistic reality, where action and reaction follows in relatively quick succession, we are still extremely slow to learn. Barring accidents, evolution proceeds at snail's pace (no offence to gastropod mollusks intended either). Maybe it's a sort of remnant of total luck of responsibility we exhibited when romping around, skinless, in the Garden of Eden. No wonder the Lord dressed us and told us to pull up our socks. Or our sense of responsibility. Alas, freedom comes with responsibility, and responsibility cannot be exercised without free will.

It's as simple as that!

But there is an even greater need for the indestructibility of matter: latent intelligence present in all animals, fish, birds, bugs, trees. In all of flora and fauna. The potential is there, in every atom. In time, in a billion years or two, these seeds of intelligence will also grow in understanding. After all, we did. Didn't we?

Surely, after a few billions of years...

The worst is yet to come.

Humanity is steeped in countless religions that advocate prayer. Rather than learning the code of behavior, rather than developing our intelligence, we are told to pray. Not in gratitude for the splendor of the world around us, but to pray for more. Why make an effort when the Lord can do it for us effortlessly? Isn't He almighty? Isn't it easy for Him? Why shouldn't He cure me of all my ills, repair the damage I've done? What of Infinite Compassion, Love, and all that...?

I read about a present day avatar, Sai Baba, living and teaching in India. A woman left her husband dying of cancer to make the hard pilgrimage to Sai Baba and ask him for the cure. On the day she finally reached the Guru, her husband was healed. Total, absolute remission certified by a number of fully accredited physicians. Her husband died a year later.

Of cancer.

I mentioned the Law of Non-interference. God, through his emissaries, can eliminate the symptoms, but would never take free will out of the equation. Our bodies are the cumulative "symptoms" of the state of our mind. Whatever the man did which originally caused cancer, he continued doing. He paid the price regardless of having been given a second chance. Sai Baba cannot refuse a supplicatory prayer. He also cannot change the laws of the universe. These laws do not concern themselves with matter. Matter can be repaired, recycled endlessly. Nothing ever disappears from this world, it just changes form. Nothing material that is. Only our weaknesses, stupidity, laziness, and other countless signs of immaturity will ultimately cease. In a way, that's rather an easy order. We are endowed with Free Will. Neither God nor man can ever interfere with our autonomy—not unless we let them. Whatever we do we shall either pay for or reap the benefits from. That's guaranteed. And as for our weaknesses, well, they were not real to start with.

They live only in our imagination, in the belief in our limitations.

That's a transient condition. Our true self is indestructible.
Like matter.
Like Spirit.

***

001216

FOOTNOTES

(1). It is accepted in Hinduism, Buddhism and Jainism.
(2). "Unto Adam also and to his wife did the Lord God make coats of skins, and clothed them." Gen.3:21

Hence the man of virtue takes charge of the tally;
The man without virtue takes charge of exaction.
It is the way of heaven to have no favorites:
It is constantly on the side of the good man.

Lao-Tzu
TE CHING
Translation by D.C.Lau
[Publ. Alfred A.Knopf, Inc. 1994; part of section 44]

25

SERVICE

Rereading the Bhagavad-Gita, I was reminded of a fundamental truth that, like all truth, is self evident, yet almost invariably forgotten. I have no desire to influence the readers with the intricacies of Eastern philosophies, other then to call their attention to the great similarity of a truism recorded in the New Testament.

The truth I am referring to is, of course, Service.

Once again it struck me that the knowledge we can extract from the various scriptures is nothing more but the conclusions reached by inspired men. They are conclusions affecting the quality of our everyday life. They have nothing to do with any theologies or religious doctrines, but just, pure and simple, advise us on living in such a way as to give us the optimum pleasure, contentment, joy, and eventually—bliss of transcendent freedom. Whether we shall achieve these objectives in a physical or spiritual body, this alone is the domain of theological or religious speculation. The truth holds true in every realm.

Saul of Taurus who became known as Saint Paul must have learned a great deal at the feet of Gamaliel. But it would have done him little good had he not also learned to listen, first and foremost, to his own inner voice. I die daily, he said, meaning that he was prepared to give up all his *acquired* knowledge, should his inner voice dictate such a course. Regardless of the teaching of learned scholars, even of scriptures, he was prepared to start, daily, literally from scratch. And this could not have been easy for one steeped in the almost overpowering richness of Jewish tradition.

What has this to do with service?

Well, it depends whom or what we wish to serve. Paul decided to serve only one Master, the One abiding within his own being. He recognized no other authority. He listened politely to Peter and other apostles, but he would not allow any intermediaries between his conscience and himself. Note that Paul's attitude is not made available to any member of any of today's orthodox religions. Yet when it came to a crunch, Paul's own inner voice ruled. In this way he committed himself to *total* service.

Today, we imagine that we serve no masters, but we do.

We inherit a karmic baggage infused in our genes. Then our parents control our hearts, minds and even minor aspects of our everyday lives. Later we carry out the instructions of teachers in various schools, followed by bowing to authoritative professors at institutions of higher learning. Finally we pay homage in the form of innumerable taxes to various levels of governments and their political emissaries. All in all, we are brought up and maintained in a strict code of service. Concurrently we bend our knees to the implicit or explicit commands of various preachers, priests, imams, church elders or organizations claiming to have authority from God.

Yet, in a strange way, our masters are also performing a service to us.

The parents, teachers and professors work, often long hours, to feed us and teach us, to pass on whatever they've learned in their youth. The politicians must convince their citizen that the service they offer to provide is good enough for us to re-elect them. And the sacerdotal masters, likewise, assure us of their indispensability. We are inundated in services—we reciprocate in kind.

We all are masters *and* minions. We offer and receive service.

Of course, Paul did not have our advantages. In his days there had been no churches, no priests or bishops who could advise him. He certainly respected the services offered and expected by secular rulers, but not enough to keep him out of jail. A Hebrew, alone in a strange country, he did the best he could. His system worked. Virtually single-handed he built an organization which, until bishop Irenaeus went on a rampage against the Gnostics, followed quite closely the teaching that Paul had learned listening to his heart. Yet, the system doesn't always work. We tend to forget that our heart can also be the source of all the wrong answers.

And now we've come a full circle.

I trust I have already demonstrated that service is the primary, unavoidable, concomitant of our lives. It cannot be avoided. We can change our masters, change our allegiances, nationalities, religions, but we cannot stop receiving and rendering a service. If we do, we die. Pure and simple. Service is as necessary to survival as breathing, drinking and eating. And since it is unavoidable, it is of vital importance to decide whom or what we wish to serve. Unless we take time and trouble to define the attributes of the master(s) we are willing to serve, all is lost. Few people realize how uncompromising is the gift of free will. If we decide to serve wholeheartedly a monster, all our efforts will be directed towards this end. History is peppered with such misguided choices. Such ignorance is still rampant, today.

To repeat again, we alone decide whom or what we serve.

A hard nut to grind?
Not at all.
The answer is as simple as all the guidelines left us by the great Masters. They all say that, at the very ground level of being, you and I must serve our own Self, to the exclusion of all other. But... and here's the rub, to serve our own Self, we *must discover who we are*.

Back to Paul.

He never met the man he claimed was his Master, yet he called him Lord, the most oft word used in the Old and New Testaments. Who is this Lord? I shall answer this question with the words of the late Charles Fillmore: *So whenever you read the word Lord in Scripture say I AM instead and you will get a clearer understanding of what Jehovah is.*[1] Paul knew that. He relied on I AM from the moment he met his inner Self on the road to Damascus. And he never looked back.

Finally, there is another secret I wish to share with you. If you choose to serve I AM, you serve this very same Presence in every other person you meet. I AM is ubiquitous, IT is the universal individualized state of consciousness (no, this is not an oxymoron). And if service is anchored in loving, then you will love this very same Master in every man, woman and child you meet along your way. In your friend and neighbor, in your enemy.

At least, that's what the Scriptures say.

It's that simple.

***

001218

FOOTNOTES

(1). METAPHYSICAL BIBLE DICTIONARY [Unity School of Christianity, Unity Village, Mo., 1931]

Thou shalt have no other gods before me.
...thou shalt worship no other god:
for the Lord, whose name is Jealous, is a jealous God

Exodus
20:3 and 34:14

26

THE MASTER

Even before I wrote my essay on *Service*, some of my friends could not reconcile the concept of the Master without conjuring an image of an exulted ego. The Christian orthodox religious people particularly found the worship of, or service to, the Self, well... sort of self-serving.

When they're right, they're right!

But just before we discard the concept of the Master as suggested by the more esoteric interpretation of the various Scriptures, let us examine the concept in greater detail. The matter is not quite as simple as we would like but let us try.

The (Inner) Master is a spiritual concept of Perfection. In a way, IT (He)[1] is the Personification of whatever divine attributes we are capable of imagining. Our imagination does not limit the Master, but it does limit our understanding of Him, or of the realization of this sublime state of Consciousness. As we grow, our Concept growth, even as the physical universe expands in direct proportion to our ability to encompass infinity. However, the particular universe we live in, in its present form, is transient. We know that even the largest stars are said to have a limited lifespan, albeit counted in billions of years. Yet even they, once their hydrogen and helium burns out, are destined to collapse and explode, some to continue to collapse into neutron stars, or even into the enigmatic black holes.

The Master is not subject to fluctuations of any nature.

To reiterate, the Master, the I AM, is a spiritual concept. As such IT has Its being outside the confines of time. Yet by regarding I AM within the framework of time, we are able to arrange an infinity of events in a sequential order. With our spiritual eyes, we can discern as the Master, the Ultimate State of Consciousness, observes dispassionately the stars exploding in magnificent fanfares, and then guides the convoluting clouds of matter and energy into new formations, new stars and planets, in which, in the fullness of time, new biological forms will once again allow the Consciousness to partake in the act of becoming.

The Master is also outside the limitation of space.

IT (or He) is present simultaneously everywhere. By imposing constrains of space, we place our attention on *particular* aspects of the Infinite, yet He remains irreducible and ubiquitous. He manifests His Consciousness through the countless units of awareness even as we manifest our consciousness through the trillions of biological cells. The Master, or the High Self, is a state of Consciousness which is ever absorbing, as though through a universal mirror, our growing understanding of Its infinite potential. What limits Its manifestation, again, is our puny realization of Its true nature. But the Master is equally present in you as in me, as in the evolving consciousness in the most distant star on the fringes of the furthest galaxy. Again, what limits Its (His) reality in the realm of becoming (the physical consciousness) is our inability to fathom Its (His) true nature.

The Hindus call Him Krishna, the Supreme Personality of Godhead. The Christians call Him the Christ. He is the personification of the Divine State of Consciousness—a statement bordering on the meaningless, as no human being can ever embrace such a concept fully. But what we can and must do, is to try hard to grow in the realization of our minuscule yet indivisible and indispensable part of the Whole. Although we shall never encompass even this concept with our intellect, we must, in the initial stages, employ our imagination, our mind and our feelings (the potential of our emotional nature) to accomplish this end. Eventually we shall arrive at a transcendental understanding that is far beyond the intellectual comprehension—even as Mozart's Requiem is beyond the hysterical amp-inflated, drug-induced atonal thumping of a disgruntled rock star.

Throughout time, the Master, the I AM, remains unchanged.

It is not because the act of becoming is an abortive or futile exercise (it is an act of infinite love). In fact, the act of becoming, what we call 'life', is an attempt by the Infinite to share Its attributes with that which is finite. With you and me. Nevertheless, I AM, being outside time and space, is already everything IT ever was or ever could be. IT, or He, was neither born nor is capable of death. The Immortal Potential of the universe is always available to share Its bounty. It is as though the Master created countless mirrors in which to contemplate His own being.

And thus, when we serve our Master, our High Self, we serve not that which we imagine our ego will one day become; rather we announce the day when we shall rise above and dispense with our ego and assume conscious identity of our true Self. When we try to identify with the I AM, we serve that which is the source of our awareness of being and becoming because, at the heart of our Consciousness, we are both, being and becoming. We are the Cause and the Effect. We embody our reality.

The practitioners of various orthodox religions needn't worry.

We, who attempt to pay homage, to express our love and serve our Master, the High Self, do not equate our nature with some lesser gods. Nor do we imagine that we shall ever become gods. What we do hope and strive to achieve, is the ever growing realization of who we really are. And this too is not for our personal glory. Should we achieve Self-Realization, we will have become aware of being made of the very same ineffable fabric as that which we call God. We shall achieve understanding of what it really means to be an indivisible fragment of the Infinite... of infinite Love... of ultimate Order, Harmony and Beauty.

On that day our real life shall begin. And from that day on we shall submerge in full consciousness in the Ocean of Infinite Possibilities.

And from that day on we shall bathe in Bliss.

***

001219

FOOTNOTES

(1). I often prefer the use of IT rather than He. IT, with both letters capitalized, represents not neutral but hermaphroditic concept. It is neither male nor female – IT is both.

– *Then you are God...?*

"First you have to understand yourself.
I told you that. And then you will understand me.
I'm not a man, I'm not a woman.
I'm not old. I'm not young.
I'm all of these."

In conversation with
Sai Baba
Schulman, Arnold BABA
[Simon & Schuster, Canada 1971; pg. 176]

27

SACRIFICES

From the day our hairy and hoary ancestors slaughtered innocent animals to appease the Big Juju lest He or She might mete out justice upon their guilty heads, sacrifice remained a favorite pastime for the practitioners of most world religions. From little lambs smoked over a ceremonial fire, through the blood initiations of the descendants of the Egyptian hierophants who offered their lives for the past, present and future sins of mankind, to Paul's enumeration, in his letters to the Hebrews, of bloody sacrifices of bulls, calves, goats and heifers, and his final assurances that: were *a testament is, there must also of necessity be the death of the testator.*[1] Blood galore, throughout the ages, oozing from every pore.

Not much has changed. The Big Juju remained unappeased.

Later, religions that regarded themselves more progressive, more suitable for modern, putatively intelligent men, tried hard to convert this deep psychosis to a more palatable rite. Nevertheless, all three of the world's most populous religions, the Hindûs, the Christians and the Moslem, continue to advocate sacrifices, in various forms, as a legitimate method of earning eternal redemption.

Isn't it time to give up such primitive notions?

Does anyone really still believe that God would take time from His busy schedule to accord reward or punishment on anyone guilty or not guilty of indulging in sacrificial offerings? Do people really still believe heaven to be a geographical location, never verified, never offered on the organized tour circuit, never affirmed in, say, the last three million years of evolution by anyone, *absolutely anyone*, who's been there, seen it, liked it, and came back to tell the story?

Silence? Not one person—man, woman, or child?

Heaven exists. It is vital, fantastic, marvelous, indescribable, endless, eternal, inexhaustible, resplendent in euphoric bliss. But it is not a place! You don't *go* there. Neither now nor after a spurious death. Neither can heaven be entered as a result of sacrifice, fasting, prayer, ritualistic offerings, drinking of blood or any other religious cocktail.

Heaven is a state of mind.

It must be realized.

It exists within us. Once realized, it opens its gates to a realm that floods our awareness both, within and without. But we don't 'go' *up* to 'go' to heaven. We go *in*. Inside our own state of consciousness. That's where God is. That's where all things are possible. That's where there is no sacrifice, no pain, no "giving up", no hardship imposed by any religious regime. It is a state of Bliss resulting from an implicit awareness of infinite Peace, Love, and Beauty as well as an awareness of absolute freedom not hampered by any limitations.

To repeat, heaven must be *realized.*

Yet within the magnificent Islam philosophy of submission to the Highest Attributes within us, there are those who still encourage gullible youths to sacrifice their bodies in an act of premeditated murder in order to reach this ineffable state of consciousness. Other imams advocate withdrawal from 'worldly' pleasures, which, are we to assume, must have been created by the Almighty for the sole use of unworthy sinners?

And the Moslems are not alone.

The Hindu swamis also encourage their acolytes to sacrifice all sensual pleasures in order to free themselves from the cycle of reincarnation. When will they realize that the Universe is the Personification of God? That God's thoughts are manifested in all that our senses can experience? That reincarnation enables us to partake in the feast that God prepared for us? I don't deny that there may well be other, probably countless, states of consciousness in which we can express differently our admiration for the beauty of creation. There may well be other planets, other esoteric forms of existence that will be ours in some distant future. Perhaps one day we shall move about unencumbered by physical, aging bodies. Perhaps we shall whisk about from star to star, from galaxy to galaxy in search of new, unimaginable experiences. Who knows?

But is this a reason to despise the gift of life now in our grasp?

Soul lives in the present.

Must we sacrifice life in order to gain life? And what of the reputedly 'future' life in some religious heaven? Shall we be called upon, by some other priesthood with a neurotic bent for sacrifice, to give up that life also? Even the sacrificially minded Hindû commentator, the renowned A.C Bhaktivedanta, admits that he, who eliminates duality from his mind, "is liberated—*even in this material world.*"[2]

True, the Christ had said that we should give up life in order to gain life. But it is the life of sacrifice, of blindness, superstition, of belief in and attachment to limitations, of disbelief that happiness is a state of mind (or better still a state of consciousness) that we must give up. He also said *My yoke is easy, and my burden is light.*[3] Not filled with theological riddles, with litanies of morals, commandments, rules and obligations, thousands of dos and don'ts... but *easy.*

Of course we shouldn't become attached to material goods and comforts. Were we to do so, their loss would upset our happiness. But for as long as we are blessed with the bounty of the Lord, let us enjoy it, let us express gratitude and enjoy it to the full. That's what it's for. For you and me. Now.

And then there are the Catholics.

The last I heard, they were still encouraged to give up God's blessings. Sweets for lent, some joys or pleasures as offering for a desired healing, the comfort of home to attend mass on a day of blizzard. Isn't God everywhere? Can Catholics, and other Christians for that matter, find Him only in a place of worship? Whatever happened to "*...when thou prayest, enter into thy closet, and when thou has shut thy door, pray to thy Father...*"[4] Can't they worship God absolutely everywhere not just in a church? St. Francis of Assisi did. And can't they serve their God all the time, not just on a Sunday? With thanks, not just with constant requests, demands, begging? I am sure some do, but most? Are most satisfied with their lot in life? Are they full of joy? By all means they should retire to a place which facilitates greater realization of the blessings around them. If they find such conditions in a church, so be it. But the purpose of the trip must be to go *in*, not to go *out*, no matter how sacrificial the trip! When will the Catholics realize that not the church but their *consciousness* is their true haven, their port of refuge, in which they create reality?

And even the very principle of the Holy Mass...

Don't they call it also a Bloodless *Sacrifice*? How dare they sacrifice another person's body and blood, even in a symbolic form, for their own misbegotten errors? Hasn't the Christ done enough for them by showing them the Way? The way to live, the way to freedom, the way to liberation and happiness? And if they claim, as some do, that the Mass is *only* a commemoration, don't they know that soul has its being *only* in the present?

We mustn't wait to go to heaven. We may loose the way...

The only things we must sacrifice are our blindness, our belief in limitations, and our attachment to transiency of matter. What if matter will dissolve after a while? We don't. We are eternal. We always have been. We always shall be.

***
001220

FOOTNOTES

(1). Hebrews 9:13 - 16
(2). BHAGAVAD-GITA AS IT IS, translations and purports by His Divine Grace A.C.Bhaktivedanta Swami Prabhupada [The Bhadtivedanta Book Trust, Los Angels 1972] pg. 91. My emphasis.
(3). Matthew 11:30
(4). Matthew 6:6

I am where My servant thinks of Me.
Every servant has an image of Me;
whatever image my servant forms of Me,
here I will be.

I am the servant of My servant's image of Me.
Be careful then, My servants, and purify, attune,
and expand your thoughts about Me.
For they are My House.

Jalal-ud-Din Rumi
Harvey, Andrew LIGHT UPON LIGHT
Inspirations from RUMI
[North Atlantic Books, Berkeley, California 1996; pg. 131]
Excerpt from *The Truth Is within You*

28

HELLO?

Are you there...?
I am always here.
Ahhh.
Yes? What is it?
I was wandering...
You have no secrets before Me.
Yeah, I know. Well, I was wondering, could you help me lose weight?
Why?
People tell me... well, I'm told that I'm considerably overweight.
I meant, why do you want Me to help you.
You are the Almighty. You can do anything.
And you can't?
Apparently.
I am under a distinct impression that I gave you free will. Have you tried abstaining from food?
What, altogether? Surely, I would promptly die! You know I can't do that!
I don't eat.
Ha, Ha! You are...
Yes I know. But have you tried? There were others before you who succeeded.
Then why can't I?
Are you asking me?
You're omniscient.
Thanks for reminding me. You can do anything you want.
You're kidding!

I never kid.
I thought laughter was a divine trait.
Only among humans. You laugh when you are happy but that's a different kind of laughter—it's often quite silent. Laughter also helps you not to take yourselves too seriously. Often you use it to cover up your mistakes.
I never thought of it that way... But laughter is O.K., isn't it?
Much better than tears.
Ha! Ha!
There you go. You are covering up not knowing the obvious.
About this weight business. Can I rally do it on my own? I have tried, you know.
I am omniscient.
Haaa.... I know... I am covering up... Well, can't you help me just a little bit?
I gave you a well-organized body, imagination, mind and consciousness. Isn't that help enough?
You really think I can do it on my own?
You never do anything on your own. I am always with you.
Then...?
You tend to forget that.
But if you are always with me, then, surely, nothing is impossible!
I think the appropriate comment is ha, ha.
Good God!
Yes?
No, I meant...
I know.

Shall I ever learn to use the powers you gave me?
Ever is a long time.
It's going to take a while...
Time doesn't really exist. It's a question of faith.
You mean if I believe...

Everything is possible. Faith is not for the intangible. Next to Love, it is the most powerful force in My universe.
But I must believe in You! You are intangible!
Am I? Look around you. I am in everything you see, hear, smell, feel, in every atom and subatomic particle. I penetrate your every thought, feeling, every desire. There is nothing that is not of Me.
But.....
I carry the universe on my shoulders. And I made you in My image.
So if I really believe I can loose weight?
You can do anything.
Like a god?
Not quite.
I thought the prophets said ye are gods!?
When you learn to do all the things I do, you shall be Me.
You mean I shall be Me.
That's what I said.

Hello?
Yes?
Thank you.

***

001221

*If ye have faith as a grain of mustard seed,
ye shall say unto this mountain,
Remove hence to yonder place;
and it shall remove;*

and nothing shall be impossible unto you

Matthew 17:20

29

THE GOD PARTICLE

Some people are still subscribing to the absurd idea that those who withdraw from life serve God better than those who swim in the midst of its often turbulent, often seemingly capricious, currents. What utter balderdash (I like this word!). I'd rather say that those who can't or are unwilling to swim should get out of the pool, or at least move to a slower lane. Otherwise, they are likely to slow down those who are willing to swim let alone impede our fun.

But fun notwithstanding, those who have awakened to the fact that they are alive, (most have not), dedicate at least some of their time to the unmasking of who or what they are. In as much as those who withdraw from life, for whatever reason, may well have more time for theoretical or perhaps transcendental meditations, I strongly suspect that, at least recently, in the department of self-realization the scientific fraternity leave the members of most sacerdotal communities well behind.

There are two basic ways to learn about what makes us (and the universe) tick.

One is to observe the effects. In this group people hope to arrive at some knowledge of the cause, perhaps Prime Cause (the pre-big-bang cosmic egg?), by studying the effects of the big-bang. They usually assume that the initial cause is either unknowable or at the very least speculative, whereas the *effects,* of whatever the cause, might shed light, sooner or later, on the motivating impulse. There are both scientists and theologians in this group, though the scientists are usually more honest in their aspirations. Generally, we can call the members of this group *phenomenalists,* or people concerned with understanding reality by the study of whatever is discernible to or by our senses.

The second group is more concerned with the motivating force behind the events, rather than the effects (events) themselves. They don't care so much *how* anything happens as *why*. In the past, the pure scientist would call such people speculators, poets or mystics. Yet by attempting to arrive at the perception of reality by intellectual intuition the members of this second group free themselves from obvious subjectivity which senses impose on their perception of reality. Furthermore, quantum theory attests that the very act of observation may affect some of the characteristics of the observable data, or at least make them selective.(1) Emmanuel Kant named this intellectual pursuit *noumenalism* from the Greek word *noumenon* meaning anything perceived by mind rather than by senses.(2)

If we ignore the fundamentalist and/or creationist crackpots who reject both: the evidence of their senses and their mind, then we are left, one would think, with the race between the phenomenalists (scientists) and the noumenalists (philosophers/theologians).

Right?

Not so.

There was a time when the two groups have been oceans, one could say light-years, apart. No more. Theoretical physicists' speculations on virtual reality are worthy of the best suppositions promulgated by the best noumenalists. Contrarily, our present pope, His Holiness John-Paul II, the leader of the most populous *religion*, is a self-avowed phenomenalist. The book *THE ACTING PERSON* which he co-authored with Dr. Anna-Teresa Tymieniecka, asserts his philosophy. On the other hand, another book written by Leon Lederman, an experimental physicist, Nobel laureate, director of the Fermi National Accelerator Laboratory from 1979 to 1989, and chairman of the board of the American Association for the Advancement of Science, is entitled *THE GOD PARTICLE*.(3) In it, Lederman 'speculates' that eventually we shall find a particle so small, as to be *really* indivisible, the original Greek meaning of a-tom. Understanding the nature of such a particle will enable us, he hopes, to understand the nature of the Universe. It may be of some interest that the days when atom was assumed the smallest particle have been displaced by an army of quarks, leptons and bosons, one could say generations smaller than the atom. It should also be duly noted that Lederman is an avowed experimentalist, and thus must be placed squarely on the phenomenalists' side. Now, this wouldn't be of a particular interest to the noumenalists, if it weren't for a stunning assertion by His Divine Grace A.C. Bhaktivedanta Swami Prabhupada who, in his commentary to BHAGAVAD GITA, the Hindu scripture, states:

"Krsna (Sanskrit for Krishna)... the supreme controller of the universe... is smaller than the smallest. The living entity is one ten-thousandth the tip of a hair in size, but the Lord is so inconceivably small that He enters into the heart of this particle."(4)

The God particle? We must ask Dr. Lederman.

It seems that there are still but two types of people in the world. Those whom the Christ called "the dead", and those who are interested in pursuing the Truth. By whatever the method—to whatever end. Both phenomenalists and noumenalists do their best, or at least try to do their best, towards the discovery of the God Particle. Perhaps both will be more successful when they center their efforts a little less on the macro- and a little more on the micro-universe. It seems to me that if (depending on religious convictions) the Buddha, Krishna and Christ all reside within us, then we, you and I, might be a good place to start our research. Both in the phenomenal and noumenal way. It may be less exciting, but might prove more beneficial and rewarding in the long run. After all, is it really wise to assume that *all* the Avatars of the past have been wrong? While we take time to decide with which group to bind our efforts, we can be sure of one thing above all others. Whoever does nothing to discover True Reality, will forever remain in the darkness. *Self*-realization is, by definition, an individual search. The dead will remain the dead. By choice. Like most people. Thank heaven for the selfish gene!

***
001226

FOOTNOTES

(1). see footnote #55 in *Why the Fall*, hereinbefore.
(2). *Noumenon* in turn from neut. of *noumenos*, ppr.pass. of *noein*, to perceive, from *noos*, the mind. [WEBSTER'S DICTIONARY]
(3). Lederman, Leon THE GOD PARTICLE with Dick Teresi, [Houghton Mifflin Co. New York 1993]
(4). BHAGAVAD-GITA AS IT IS, translations and purports by His Divine Grace A.C. Bhaktivedanta Swami Prabhupada [The Bhaktivedanta Book Trust, Los Angeles 1968, 1972] page 144. It should be noted that Bhagavad-Gita also asserts that soul pervades the whole body. It is thus evident that soul fits nicely into the concept of quantum physics, evidently consisting of innumerable quanta.

Nothing exists except atoms and empty space; everything else is opinion.

Democritus of Abdera
430 B.C.

30

HEAVEN AND HELL

Recently I've revisited my old friend Aldous Huxley. Not that I've ever actually met the gentleman, but after reading his Brave New World and some of his other ventures into the realm of imagination, I thought I knew what to expect from him.

I was wrong.

In his *Doors of Perception* and *Heaven and Hell*(1) he not only surprised me, but, I regret to say, left me quite disappointed. Not by his personal experiments with mescaline and other drugs, but by his apparent desire to equate the artificial effects, or any effects for that matter, with the Reality he quite obviously had been searching. The same error has been quite blatantly committed later by Castaneda in his Don Juan series.(2)

Periodically we meet other experimenters, such as Timothy Leary, whose LSD trips are known to have been very successful in leading absolutely nowhere.(3) I find it quite fascinating that in spite of repeated failures to substitute synthetic results for the real thing the new waves of misguided aspirants never manifested in such numbers as in our present drug-laden generation. It seems that those who partake in such futile exercises are not really searching for a new reality, but rather endeavor to escape the reality of their lives, which appear to be devoid of anything worthwhile. Furthermore, while the euphoric states achieved by such means are eminently artificial, the antipodal hells are reputed to be very real.

Artificial or real, both suffer from transient results.

This misguided search for a different reality is all the more abortive since it misses both proven methods of widening one's horizons without sacrificing one's sanity. It is quite true that mescaline, carbon dioxide, LSD and other shamanic entheogens induce various 'unearthly' experiences in our brains and sensory systems under the guise of "exploration of spiritual growth." I suggest that the reason is that all externally applied methods strive to empower man to the limits of his physical potential, rather than to free him from his inherent bodily limitations imposed by the senses. For as long as we see ourselves as men endowed with latent divine abilities, we are destined for a painful dead end. I am not aware of any examples to the contrary.

If so, why bother? Why travel a road that leads nowhere?

There are two methods which, rather than dwelling on our limited material potential, expand our horizons in quite a different 'direction'. The interpreters of some eastern philosophies, particularly of the Bhagavad-Gita and other Vedic texts favor the first method. Those interpretations rely on attaching ourselves to the coattails of the Supreme Master, the Super Soul, whom the designated Swamis call (among countless other names), the Personality of Godhead. This Personality resides in all living creatures, and constant mental vigilance, service, and adoration of this Inner/Outer Divinity assures us of eventual rise into the realm of transcendental bliss.

The second method of expanding our consciousness is, it could be said, quite the opposite. If the first can be called *devotional*, than the second, the one that I espouse, would be called *contemplative*. This is neither the time nor have we the space to expound at length on the subject in hand, other than to refer an interested reader to the works by Meister Eckhart, to a lesser degree Thomas Morton, some exponents of Sufism such as Jalaludin Rumi, as well as to a number of other mystics.(4) The paradigm of this method is, of course, Jesus Christ who, in the final phase of his temporal existence could

HEAVEN AND HELL

no longer distinguish between himself and the object of his contemplation. What really matters is that neither of the two methods relies on the expansion of our physical potential, but rather on sublimating our physical nature to our true or real state of being. This in no way denies living life to the full, but merely transfers our consciousness from sensual to spiritual. This is accomplished by, as the Moslem would say, submitting to the Highest. The question that separates the two methods lies in where do we place this Highest. Those who have the need to adore, to serve, place divinity squarely outside their own being and serve what they believe will, one day, assure them of 'heaven' in whatever form.

The second, the contemplative, method is very different.

It assumes that the ubiquity of the Divine is so prevalent, so uncompromising, that it already exists in Its full Majesty *within* our being. All we must do is to *realize* this fact. This system is not an intellectual pursuit. It is not a philosophy to be argued back and forth until some common ground is achieved. Every practitioner of the contemplative method will reach his of her realization at a different time, in a different way, to a different degree. There is no possible way to define the 'effect', as Huxley would like to call it, as the effect is the arrival at "no effect". The reality an aspirant is seeking is one wherein all effects, all conjuring tricks, have been left behind; wherein we no longer have any needs, good or bad, yet partake in all of them as observers. By sacrificing the personal traits of our individuality, we become truly *individual* or *indivisible*, in fact INDISTINGUISHABLE from the Whole, from the Universal. We partake in all that was, is, or could ever be.

There is one other major difference that separates the two methods. The devotional method implies or threatens constant escape towards some elusive ethereal state, an eventual heaven, to be achieved on liberation from the present material reality. One pursuing the contemplative method does not suffer from such conditions. Heaven is already here, everywhere, indestructible, waiting to be admitted into our awareness.

Over the last few thousand years, hundreds of tomes had been written on the subject discussed above. Regrettably, no words can lead to the experience itself. Nor can the state itself, no matter how desirable, be shared with another. The ineffable consciousness must be realized, individually—not read about. What I endeavor to do is to whet your appetite, not eat your meal for you. The table is laid... One other item should be mentioned.

Although within the realm of the Soul, when realized, we completely loose our identity within the Infinite, we do, nevertheless remain sublimely aware that it is 'I' who is lost within the All.

I AM is indestructible, even when I and my Father become reunited.

***

001230

FOOTNOTES

(1). [Penguin Books, Middlesex, England, 1971]
(2). Castaneda, Carlos THE SECOND RING OF POWER [Simon and Schuster 1979]. Also TALES OF POWER, THE TEACHINGS OF DON JUAN, et al.
(3). LSD (lysergic acid diethylmide) is a powerful hallucinogen.
(4). While one can but admire Thomas Morton's total commitment, he does, in my opinion, suffer from considerable Catholic conditioning which appears to limit his freedom.

Thou preparest a table before me...

Psalm 23:5

31

SOUL OF A MACHINE

Sometime ago I read a book entitled *Soul of a New Machine*.(1) No, the author of the Pulitzer prize-winning novel does not propose that computers have souls. He does suggest, however, that without soul, computers might not have come into being. The book came to mind after a dinner party I attended at which the lady of the house, armed with a Ph.D. in biology, expressed her opposition to cloning on the grounds that two equal cells would have to share a single soul, probably half each. Or possibly grow up to be like computers which being made of identical components would exhibit identical characteristics. I've written before on the biblical definition of soul.(2) At the risk of being exorcised as well as excommunicated by the sacerdotal fraternity, I wish to share with you my own view on the subject.

I'll start with the quote of J.B.S.Haldane: *"The universe is not only stranger than we imagine. It is stranger than we can imagine."*

While, to date, there is absolutely no evidence that there is intelligent life outside our ball of dirt, there are a hundred thousand million suns in each of a hundred thousand million galaxies. To assume that we have monopoly on the allotment of souls, by whatever definition, in a cloned or not cloned specimen of human offspring, is more than ludicrous; it is pompously if not blasphemously presumptuous. And even if we were to relegate the concept of soul to a thinking process, then let me quote another above-average member of our (otherwise priggish) species Marvin Minsky: "Can a machine think? I'm a machine, I think." While I share Minsky's view, I'm not sure Descartes would be pleased to be ranked together with a motorcar, robot, or any other automaton.

No. Thinking ability, no matter how very limited or boundless, is not the answer. Nor is the ability to compute, calculate or twiddle our noses at other species that often show greater potential than we do. Soul has nothing to do with biological, mechanical or technological evolutionary achievements.

Soul IS.

I have written in my previous essays that I define Soul as the individualization of the Omnipresent Consciousness, which our sacerdotal brethren insist on calling God. A more precise definition would be to say that Soul is the attribute adopted by the Infinite Intelligence to individualize Itself in the manifested universe as Consciousness. This attribute may or may not be maintained in the unmanifested reality but, since we have no way of knowing, I shall leave such speculations to professional theologians.

Thus there is neither one soul controlling, yet limited to, two cloned entities of human or any other species or extraction, nor are there two souls imbedded in each of the thinking specimens. There is, however, One Soul, one could say an attribute of One God, manifested throughout one hundred thousand million suns in each of the one hundred thousand million galaxies, and any other universes which our illustrious astronomers or theoretical speculators have not yet brought into the open.

The next question we must ask ourselves, why would Soul choose to manifest Itself in or through a sycophant species on a backward planet of a near-average sun?

A good question indeed.

It seems that Soul, in Its magnificent magnanimity, will provide such degree of consciousness as the object of Its attention can absorb. Thus a stupid, selfish, complacent person will manifest a different degree of Soul than his or her opposite. We all know the expression Mahatma, meaning Great Soul. Of course, Soul is great, in fact infinite. What defines Its apparent greatness is the inherent ability and willingness of the instrument through which Soul manifests Itself. Thus Soul could do nothing through Mozart's entity, should Mozart refuse to compose. It could do nothing through Jesus, should Jesus refuse to carry out His mission. The same is true of every one of us. Of you and me.

But let us not be so foolish as to presume that Soul would refuse to experience the manifested universe through any non-human, non-biological, non-pigheaded instrument, willing and ready to receive a gift of a marginally more advanced state of consciousness. I say, "marginally more advanced" because Soul enlivens all animals, all birds and fish, bugs, viruses, even as plants, bushes and trees. And if such an instrument were made of identical atoms born in the fiery heart of the same distant star but arranged in a different, what some might call, mechanical form, so be it. The realization of the Soul's presence might differ, but, let's face it, how many human entities do you know who enjoy a deep realization of being an instrument through which God, by the miracle of Soul, experiences the joy of becoming?

***
010101

FOOTNOTES

(1). Tracy Kidder, SOUL OF A NEW MACHINE [Avon Books, New York 1981]

(2). BEYOND RELIGION Volume I, *Body and Soul* (961203), [Inhousepress, Montreal 1997, 2001, Amazon Kindle Edition 2010]

32

SKIMMING THE SURFACE

This morning's daily paper reported that the Cambodia's National Assembly approved the creation of a tribunal to prosecute the leaders of the Maoist leaders of the Khmer Rouge for their crimes, including the murder of 1.7 million peasants. It would be interesting to see how does one impose justice on a murderer of so many? Alas, the impending prosecution is too late to mete justice on most of the leaders of the homicidal clique, including Pol Pot himself, who died in 1998, escaping his just deserts.

Or did he?

According to all people who skim the surface of reality—he did. According to them, therefore, we can do all we want, at whosoever's expense, providing we can get away with it by dying in the nick of time.

So far so good. But... what if....?

What if the sages of the past had been right? What if there is such a thing as reincarnation and the attendant karma? What if the 'speculations' of our long passed predecessors are no less right than those of our theoretical physicists who postulate theories many of which are *not* proven experimentally to this day? And the theories of the latter day's prophets, those sporting a string of Ph.D.s after their names, are a lot easier to prove than the theories proposed by the scientists of yore.

Are we to dismiss hypotheses of theoretical cosmologists simply because, by skimming the surface, we cannot understand them? Richard Feynman, in one of his lectures on the quantum theory, advised his listeners not to take his: "...lecture too seriously." That if we questioned "how can (the universe) be like that?" we would end up in "a blind alley from which nobody has yet escaped."[1] Feynman was referring to physics, not metaphysics. Shall we take his advice and wallow in our, so jealously guarded, ignorance? Most people choose just that. Whether it concerns their body, mind or soul, most people are more than willing to skim the surface of reality, never venturing into the deep, the unknown, the unexplored territory, lest they be accused of *escaping* from an imitation reality that serves them as a substitute for Truth.

Most of us are happy to skim the surface.

There are also other surface skimmers. They are the people who know practically everything about practically nothing. They drive a wedge so thin, as to disfigure the image of reality completely. Little wonder. The scholarship of human genius became so vast that the only way in which inferior minds can make a living (other than playing a professional sport or strumming an amplified guitar) is to narrow their specialization to such a degree that in their extremely narrow field they can teach others about... practically nothing. Imagine an artist limiting him/her self to one or two colors. Or one or two geometric shapes. What would be your opinion of them? Yet how would such pseudo artists differ from the illustrious professors lecturing at institutions of high learning, where they impose their most narrow of views on minds not yet strangled by irons of specialization?[2] I would like to see a Ph.D. being awarded to people who write a thesis on five divergent subjects. Or who substantiate their theories by referring their proposals to five divergent segments of our lives. Or who describe the beauty of an atom's structure, perhaps the music of the vibrating strings of which it is (possibly) made and not just its sub nuclear elements in mathematical terms. Rather as Feynman

also implied: *"If you will simply admit that maybe (nature) does behave like this, you will find her a delightful, entrancing thing."*
Delightful, entrancing thing.
And Feynman was speaking about quantum mechanics! About the invisible, the infinite, the virtually impalpable, the often unprovable, the delightful, the entrancing... Rather like speaking about God. Or about, what Leon Lederman called, the "God Particle."[3] Not about the invisible, the impalpable, the often unprovable, the delightful, the entrancing concept of incarnation and karma.

Not even about incarnation and karma...
Did Pol Pot really escape justice? Not if we accept our physicists' assurances that nothing ever disappears in this world, neither matter nor energy. Not a single atom of matter, nor a minute quantum of energy. The vibrations live on, interchangeable, immortal, ever regrouping, coalescing, compounding into new forms, new constructs of our delightful, entrancing reality. Pol Pot did not escape his just deserts if we accept the hard-nosed physicists' definition of infinity. If you and I and Pol Pot are, at some level of our being, also immortal, then what is there to stop Pol Pot from being reincarnated 1.7 million times and being sentenced to death in each and every life, each time innocent of the crime as had been his victims, by a corrupt judge with an inflated ego? Infinity is a long, long time...

Does it matter?
At our level of evolution it only seems to matter if it happens to us. Personally. But at a higher level, or perhaps at a level which is deeper—well below the shallow understanding we, the practical people, seem so proud of, at the level of the great mystics of past and present, we are all One. The universe is One and we are irrevocably tied to the universe in which we find the awareness of our being. At some level of this ineffable being we all partake in atoms, energies and vibrations of the universe we live in. By the

same irrevocable logic, we all partake in the national, racial and global karma. Who knows, perhaps galactic and universal also.
At some level of our being...
Forever.

***
010103

FOOTNOTES

(1). Richard Feynman Ph.D., theoretical physicist, winner of Nobel Prize in 1965 for work on quantum electrodynamics, was dubbed by Freeman Dyson: "The most original mind of his generation."

(2). Feynman mentioned above, in his essay "What is Science" warned his students to: "Learn from science that you must doubt the experts... Science is the belief in the ignorance of experts."

(3). Leon Lederman shared the Nobel Prize for physics. He was director of the Fermi National Accelerator Laboratory and the chairman of the board of the American Association for the Advancement for Science. Also see essay on *The God Particle*, hereinbefore.

*Specialist knows absolutely everything about absolutely nothing.
A generalist is the exact opposite.*

Anonymous

33

THE GREEN EYED MONSTER

I am reminded of a story I heard from a kindly old man. He said he had a vision of Hell. He saw a dark place filled with great cauldrons wherein the perpetrators of various crimes were slowly stewed in their own oil. Devils, armed with barbed tridents, surrounded virtually all the cauldrons and pushed the sinners struggling to escape their just deserts back into the simmering oil. All cauldrons except one. The pool filled with those who committed the sin of envy needed no guards. The other fryees pulled the aspiring escapees back into the oil themselves.

Such is the nature of envy.

Most of us associate envy with financial standing, power, or a prestigious position that might lead to fame. Of these, the envy of fame is probably the most insidious of all, because it is seldom if ever sublimated, let alone eradicated, by an improvement in one's own position. It relies almost entirely on the destruction of the good name of another. There had been few names in history that had not been besmirched by those who tried to elevate themselves by tarnishing the accomplishments of others. On the receiving end we can count kings and princes, renowned scientists, men of letters, poets and artists. Even saints and saviors have suffered under the bile exuded by men not worthy to untie the laces of their victims' shoes.

And envy is not limited to egos suffering from obscurity. Thomas Alva Edison held over 1300 patents. Yet his accomplishments evidently led to such an inflated ego that he fell under the spell of envy. At one time he preferred to destroy the reputation of Nikola Tesla, by spreading garrulous nonsense about the dangers of his competitor's invention—that of electric alternating-current (A/C). He laid nonsensical claims as to the efficacy of his own discovery, the direct-current, though he was already well aware of its limitations. In time Tesla was well and truly vindicated, but not before Edison drove him to near bankruptcy by his envy.

Tesla, in his turn, condemned Einstein's early achievements out of hand, without ever giving them the benefit of the doubt, let alone a serious study.

The scientist's ego is as fragile a structure as an unstable atom.

Not to be left behind, and blaming it on the principle of uncertainty, Albert Einstein virtually dismissed the theory of quantum mechanics by claiming that "God does not play dice with the universe". Coming from an acknowledged genius, a feeble argument at best. Wouldn't you say that Einstein might have been motivated, at least in part, by envy that among his peers the quantum theory was sublimating his theories of relativity?

But scientists, great and small, do not hold monopoly on envy.

Just for a moment let us consider how many careers have been ruined, how many lives laid waste, by xenophobic men and women who turned against those who did not conform to their sexual preference. Not because the small minority abused their position, not because they raped or degraded anyone as heterosexuals have done in large numbers, but because they were 'different'.

These days, however, the stigma of homosexuality is no longer enough.

The most popular method of besmirching out of jealousy and ignorance is to accuse the object of one's envy of pederasty. Since homosexuality is no longer considered an abomination but rather a result of genetic predisposition, the accusers must extend their envious ramblings to equate homosexuals, or anyone for that matter, with perverts. The line between sexual orientation and perversion is diligently erased. Thus the best way to give vent to one's envy is to accuse the (male) object of one's jealousy of sexual relations with little boys.

The armed forces are a well-known quagmire of frustrating envy. Arthur C. Clarke, the renowned writer and innovative thinker once wrote an ironic piece entitled "The Gay Warlords". Citing the Spartans, Alexander the Great, Emperor Harden, Richard the Lionhearted, and Gordon of Khartoum, Clarke suggests that the real reason the military are trying to keep homosexuals out of the army is that "they're too bloodthirsty and warlike." This, and the true story about the turn-of-the-century Commander of the Ceylon Forces, Sir Hector Macdonald VC, who rose through the ranks from private to general and was recognized as the bravest soldier of the British army, caused Clarke to pay dearly for his irony. Apparently, writes Clarke, "...to the great embarrassment of the local Brits... fighting Mac was caught *in flagrante* with some Colombo schoolboys..."(1) After the infamous event, the General promptly shot himself, and Clarke, equally as promptly, was accused of being a pederast.(2) If you can't beat them—besmirch them.

The way of envy.

The lesser the minds the lower they sink to demean those towering above them. In fact, the higher the victim the more contemptible the accuser. We all know the false accusations that led Jesus of Nazareth to the cross. Hadn't Caiaphas and his henchmen been envious of Jesus' following? Fewer know that there are modern-day pseudo-scholars who suggested Jesus also broke the biblical law by indulging in homosexuality. Who knows what a perverted mind might construe from the saying *"Suffer little children, and forbid them not, to come unto me..."*?

And on December 24, 2000, just in time for Christmas, a loving article appeared in my trusty Montreal Gazette. It reported on accusations against a modern day saint of India, a 75 year old man called Sai Baba, purportedly indulging in sexual acts with boys. In 1978 a devotee built himself an apartment in the guru's headquarters. Two decades later, after 21 years of inexplicable distraction, the devotee's eyes had been opened and he suddenly noticed that Sai Baba is a pervert. What is more, according to the accuser, Sai Baba has been enjoying his perversion with many young devotees for years and years. Only for the first 60 years or so.... no one noticed it.

This surely would be an unmatched miracle! Even for Sai Baba.

Could it be that the ex-devotee thought he deserved, after years of faithful service, a special recognition, perhaps a title, some special privileges? Could it be that he had been bypassed in the ladder of importance, by other, perhaps more humble devotees? Could it be envy? His ego scorned?

***

If we must pass judgment, then, surely, "by their fruits we shall know them." Edison gave us an incandescent lamp and many other life-enhancing gadgets. Einstein gave us a new vision of our universe and filled it with wonder beyond imagination. From Tesla we inherited the radio and alternating-current transmission. Clark gave us countless hours of enjoyable reading and stimulated our minds with dreams of what-could-be. And as for the legacy of Jesus and Sai Baba—from all that I've ever heard or read—it is a legacy of nothing but pure, unconditional love.

I envy none of them—I am grateful to all.

Envy is a green-eyed monster. But not as monstrous as the people who fall permanently under its spell. They are truly, the lost souls.

***

000105

FOOTNOTES

(1). Gleamed from the Gazette, Montreal Dec. 31,2000. Reprint of an article by Gyles Brandreth, TO 2001 AND BEYOND [London Sunday Telegraph].

(2). The award of Sir Arthur C. Clarke's Knighthood has been delayed for a year following the completely unsubstantiated accusations.

*"For eight years you were not on the earth.
Where were you? In heaven?
What is heaven?
Were you dead?
What is death?"*
"Samadhi," Baba said. *"You know this word?"*

Schulman, Arnold BABA
[Simon & Schuster, Canada 1971]

34

RUNN'N, JUMP'N & STAND'N STILL

No, I do not intend to reintroduce you to the hysterical British Goon Show.
Although...
Rather than runn'n or jump'n, most people are happiest when they're standing still. Most people congregate into little groups, rather like wolf packs, within which they wallow in a sense of security. They know that no one will say or do anything to challenge their dormant minds with a new, let alone demanding concept. They know, at all times, what to expect, what not to expect, when to smile and when to cry. The religious among them even found a word for this conformity. They called it morality, with a capital M. Whatever *We* do is moral. They or Them are immoral. They—do not conform. They are out, they don't belong.

Such groups start at the social level.

They flourish in our suburbs, in the human gestations areas, where couples move to raise young in protective surroundings, communal cocoons, wherein they do not have to worry about an untested notion disturbing the far from fulminating minds of their young. The young, in turn, are trained to be as much like their parents as possible. The girls are encouraged to play with dolls, frills and chickadees—emulating their mothers, the boys strut their meager chests, trying to look as macho as their middle-aged, frustrated, pouchy fathers. This policy holds until both sexes reach their teens.

Teens is the magic age when young'ns become aware of their wings. They stretch them a few times, tentatively, waiting for their parents to help them with the first leap. Receiving no help whatever from their partially ossified progenitors, they attempt to leap on their own. Some, wiser for no reason at all, attempt running before jumping.

It's just as hard.

Having been reared within an ultra protected environment where an original idea, thought, God forbid—behavior, were considered an unspeakable no-no, they fall flat on their fresh, young faces. Falling—without ever having fallen before—is a very painful experience. Some, to avoid such anguish give up immediately and make their parents proud by donning the uniform of uniformity. Most, however, due to the spirit that refuses to give up at the first attempt, continue running and jumping. Early upbringing makes them incapable of existing as individuals. Emulating their elders, they form groups, cliques, and gangs. New, defiant cohesion gives them strength, a sense of belonging: same clothing, hairstyle, same body piercing, and even the same senseless argot. Their parents continue to stand very still, holding their breath.

The barrier grows higher, the gulf—deeper.

Within a few months, years at most, the whimsy that motivates the teenagers becomes diametrically opposed to their parents. If the parents are dull, they become outrageous. If the parents are 'intellectuals', they assume the role of mental vegetables. If their parents are 'religious', they become atheistic. If their parents are snobs, they don jeans with as many holes torn out at oscillating beer parties as is possible without catching a cold. In other words, they become motivated rebels.

It really doesn't matter at all what they rebel against. The important thing is not to stand still. The direction they choose is almost invariably as irresponsible as they parents suggest, their leaps are as senseless as the arguments they exchange with their despairing procreators. Finally, either the despondent parents or their offspring give up.

It really doesn't matter who gives up first. The important thing is that every action must have a reaction. Remove opposition, and the animus fizzles out. There is no point, let alone fun, breaking the rules if there are no rules to break, or someone attempting to enforce them.

Bored, once again, one delinquent in a thousand weans itself from the imposed stagnation. Still 'it-self' because that what might eventually them men or women has not, as yet been established. For those who decide to remain in the conclave of ennui, the self-determination is relatively easy. They are not expected to become men or women. It suffices for them to grow into males and females. They must each find a partner, buy a house in the suburbs, settle down, get a dog, get pregnant, get another dog, get pregnant again, and become a useful members of the immediate local fraternity. It doesn't matter why or wherefore, as long as they conform to the morality of their particular group. They must obey many no-nos and their grand parents are eminently qualified to instill those into the male and female members ot the new productive unit of the new, expanding group.

All's well.

Nothing happens to roil the cesspool of stagnation. To hell with evolution. Stasis is what protects the selfish gene best. The future of humanity is assured. The new generation can tread water for about a dozen years, and then watch, haplessly and helplessly as their young begin runn'n and jump'n while it's their turn to remain standing very still.

Then, suddenly, some stupid dictator starts a war, or a meteor strikes the immediate environment, or there is a global collapse of economy or something equally untoward happens. For a little while, there is a tentative swell in the suburban pool. The members of the groups are forced to face the unpredictable. Men leave to kill the enemy, women stand up on their own feet, the children cope without constant supervision. A few of them learn, absorb, metabolize the excitement of living in an uncertain environment. Unbeknownst to them, for the first and only time they delve into spiritual life: a life of untried horizons, a gulp of the unknown. Evolution is jerked a few yards forward. And then the generals send more suburban troops to kill the opposition, the politicians sign treaties, and all gets back to normal.

To runn'n, jump'n, and standing still.

***
010108

*I am going to tell you what nature behaves like.
If you will simply admit that maybe she does behave like this,
you will find her a delightful, entrancing thing.
...nobody knows how it can be like that."*

Richard Feynman
(speaking about quantum theory)

35

WHO AM I?

I am the taste of water, the light of the sun and the moon... I am the sound in ether and the ability in man.

I am the original fragrance of the earth, and I am the light in fire. I am the life of all that lives, and I am the penances of all ascetics.

I am the original seed of all existence, the intelligence of the intelligent, and the prowess of all powerful men.

I am the strength of the strong, devoid of passion and desire.

I am the Self, seated in the hearts of all creatures. I am the beginning, the middle, and the end of all beings.

I am ever detached, seated as though neutral.

I am the source of everything; from Me the entire creation flows.

I am seated in everyone's heart, and from Me come remembrance, knowledge and forgetfulness.(1)

I am the bread of life, I am the light of the world.

I am the door: by me if any man enter in, he shall be saved and shall go in and out and find pasture.

I am the resurrection, I am the way, and the truth, and the life.(2)

I am he who was within me. Never have I suffered in any way, nor have I been distressed. I am the first-born son who was begotten. I am the beloved. I am the righteous one.

I am in the process of becoming.

I am the honored one and the scorned one. I am the silence that is incomprehensible. I am the one before whom you have been ashamed. I am strength and I am fear. I am war and peace. I am the one who has been hated everywhere. I am the one whom they call Life. I am the one whom they call Law. I am the one whom you have hidden from. I am sinless. I am the one who alone exists. (3)

I am where My servant thinks of Me. Every servant has an image of Me; whatever image my servant forms of Me, there I will be.

I am the servant of My servant's image of Me. Be careful then, My servants, and purify, attune, and expand your thoughts about Me, for they are My House.(4)

I am the Way-Guide, the Supreme Mind, the thoughts of Atum the One-God. I am with you—always and everywhere.(5)

To the sinful and vicious, I may appear to be evil.
But to the good—beneficent am I.(6)

A lamp am I to you that perceive me. A mirror am I to you that know me.(7)

I AM THAT I AM(8)

***

010110

FOOTNOTES

(1). BHAGAVAD-GITA [The Bhadtivedanta Book Trust, Los Angeles 1968,1972] 7: 8-11, 9:9, 10:8 and 20, 15:15.

(2). John 6:48, 8:12, 10:9, 11:25, 14:6.

(3). THE NAG HAMMADI LIBRARY IN ENGLISH, James M. Robinson, General Editor. [HarperSanFrancisco1978] The (First and Second) Apocalypse of James; On the Origin of the World; The Thunder, Perfect Mind.

(4). Andrew Harvey, LIGHT UPON LIGHT, inspirations from RUMI, [North Atlantic Books, Berkeley, California 1996] pg. 131, extract from *The Truth Is within You*

(5). Timothy Freke & Peter Gandy, THE HERMETICA The Lost Wisdom of the Pharaohs. [Judy Piatkus, London 1998] pg. 37 *The Initiation of Hermes*.

(6). Mizra Khan, ANSARI

(7). Apocryphal Acts of John

(8). Exodus 3:14

*We can't solve problems
by using the same kind of thinking we used
when we created them.*

*The most beautiful experience we can have,
is the mysterious.*

Albert Einstein
LIVING PHILOSOPHIES, 1931

36

VIRGINS

Virgin Islands are glorious. Warm, curvilinear, seductive, inviting, on occasion—steaming. Not all virgins are like that. Some rather than being verdant, consume all that's green in their diet. The Egyptian nature goddess Isis, is a case in point. This virgin mother of the godson Horus, is symbolized by a cow which, by the way, is sacred in India.

It's a small world.

And then, there had been ten virgins carrying lamps with and without oil who went to meet the bridegroom. We all know the story... How forgetful of five of them. Still, the wise virgins could have shared at least some of their oil with the foolish ones. Don't you think?[1] And taking of oil, have you tried the double and even triple virgin oil? And *à propos* wedding, I am sure that the priestesses, known as caryatids, straining under the weight of the entablature in Diana's temple, also never tasted the joys of Eros. Too bad... But when all is said and done, it is the maternal virginity that became *sine qua non* for the tales and myths of yesteryear.

In fact, virginal mothers abound in ancient religions.

The Hindû Holy Nari and the Egyptian Isis, correspond exactly to the Holy Mary known to us as the Holy Virgin. The Mother of Christ corresponds to the Hindû Mother of Krishna, and the Egyptian Mother of Horus. The litany of the Roman Catholic Virgins mirrors both the Hindû and the Egyptian beliefs. According to H.P Blavatsky, the list consists of seventeen individual titles bestowed on the Virgin

Mary by later worshippers.[(2)] Makes one wander if the early Christians did not borrow the list and merely reassigned it to a later version of the original.

The list is impressive.

There are titles corresponding to the Mother of God, Mother of Christ, Virgin of Virgins, Mother of Divine Grace, Virgin most chaste, Mother most pure, undefiled, inviolate, amiable and admirable; Virgin most powerful, merciful and faithful; Mirror of Justice, Seat of Wisdom, Mystical Rose, House of Gold, Morning Star, Ark of the Covenant, Queen of Heaven, *Mater Dolorosa* and Mary conceived without sin. Phew...!

The important thing is that every single title, mother or not, in all three religions, is a 100%, fully certified Virgin. By fully certified I mean that the titles are confirmed by either infallible scriptures which are invariably regarded as the indisputable and immutable Word of God, or by equally infallible successors to the original Divine Incarnation. I will not bore the reader with the Hindû and Egyptian original lists. Trust me, they exist, and if you don't, check with Blavatsky.

But that's not all.

The Holy Virgins had their own, presumably less holy, virgins. Just as the Virgin Mary claims a great number of nunneries or convents whose members swear virginal chastity till the last breath of their life; so did the Hindû Nari, as did Egyptian Isis, as did Vesta, a little later, in Rome. All Virgins worshipped by dedicated virgins. For life.

As my Sergeant Major would say... what a waste! With all the due respects, of course. But, let's face it, there must have been thousands of them, millions throughout the course of history.

What a terrible shame that all those wonderful virgins, ladies if you will, so greatly dedicated yet so greatly misunderstood the meaning of their real or assigned chastity. First of all, in our Bible, the Hebrew *bethulah*, *almah*, and the Greek *parthenos* are all translated into English as *virgins*.

Well, they might have been, but the words, both in Hebrew and Greek, mean separation, concealment, unmarried female, one put aside, *as well as* a virgin. Obviously, under the Hindû and the Egyptian influence, *virgin* won hands down.

Secondly, though I have few reports of the virility assigned to Isis[3] or Nari[4]—the Mother of Christ, later in her life, had at least four (other) children, which stretches the concept of virginity to the limit.[5] But only if you take the Bible literally, of course, as all the good fundamentalists are bound to do.

And this brings us the third point, the essence of the matter.

The Bible, and I strongly suspect all the other Scriptures, has been written in a symbolic language. The Sufis claim that the Koran has no less then seven levels of understanding. In our case, let us settle for just two.

Virginity, in biblical symbolism, means never having been unfaithful to God. The only intercourse that the virgin had never entertained was with evil. It means never having willingly nor knowingly strayed from the straight and narrow, never having compromised in matters of her relation with her own Higher Self—with the Indwelling Christ or simply with the Spirit within her. This, my friends, I firmly believe is a thousand times more difficult than maintaining physical virginity for any length of time, let alone for a lifetime. This is what made the Virgin Mary a *Holy* Mary. What made her Whole.

Finally, presumably suspecting that people might smell a rat, this is probably why Pius IX, having declared himself infallible, promptly elevated the Virgin Mary to the status of Immaculate Conception in 1854.[6] It is interesting to note how uninformed was the angel Gabriel who, in his ignorance, failed to greet Mary as a goddess, let alone a Mother of God, not to mention by any other illustrious title assigned her by her worshippers, but simply: "Blessed art thou among *women*," he said. Just among *women*, he said, not even among virgins...

Apparently even angels make mistakes. Anyway, as I've already illustrated, and to quote *the* expert on mythology himself, Joseph Campbell: "Images of virgin birth abound in the popular tales as well as in myth."[7]

***

And if you don't believe any of this, then just try the "Milk of the Celestial Virgin," also known as the Water of Phtha, *Anima Mundi,* and under some other esoteric names. I heard nothing about its gustatory titillation, but it is said to have magical powers.
Good luck.

***
000113

FOOTNOTES

(1). Matthew 25:1-4 et al.
(2). Blavatsky, H.P. ISIS UNVEILED Volume II, Theology, [Theosophical University Press, Pasadena, California 1988] pg.209.
(3). other than giving birth to Horus (sired by her husband Osiris)
(4). the Virginal Mother of Perpetual Fecundity as well as the incarnated God Vishnu....
(5). Five, if you prefer Luke 16:28 version.
(6). THE COLUMBIA VIKING DESK ENCYCLOPEDIA Third Ed. [Viking press, New York 1968]
(7). Campbell, Joseph THE HERO WITH A THOUSAND FACES [Princeton University Press, Bollingen Series XVII 1973; pg.312]

*For wrath killeth the foolish man,
and envy slayeth the silly one.*

Job 5:2

37

WHAT IF
?

What if there were no love? *If there were no inexplicable force binding us all together?*

We would feel emptiness in the gaze of a child. We could not sense the mystery of creation. We would not wish to remain immortal—drifting, detached, lonely, suspended forlorn within cold time forever...

We would never experience the joy of selfless giving. Nor would we share in the joy of forgiving. Our compassion would die, slowly, unrequited forever. So much to give, wanting, and no one to give to...

We would never wipe tears from a distraught eyelid, never raise smile on lips tight with fear, never give comfort to a total stranger. There would be no loved ones. No love and no loving. Just hollow indifference stretching ever onward...

Or, perhaps, without love there would still be grim hatred. We would despise, steadfastly, coldly unremitting. We would be as cursed demons in their fiery glory, only fire would sear our dark minds—our hearts would be missing...

What if we were omniscient, as Gods are omniscient?

If we could never err in matters of life or being? Sad loneliness would resound in our souls forever searching nothing. We could never share a new thought, new hope, new idea... never reminisce to a friend an arcane encounter. Nor could we describe to anyone a new vision, never compare dreams, marvel at new experience... Nor could we ever reach out for the unknown, the yet unnamed, mysterious.

We would never be curious since we'd all be all knowing.

We would not turn our gaze at yet an undiscovered country, never wonder of beauty beyond forbidden mountain. Nor would we ever marvel at secrets shrouded in antiquity, nor raise a curious eyebrow at the yet unrealized future. We would never read a new book, foreknowing all the outcomes, never recite a poem, nor study the great Masters. Nor would we ever pray for knowledge, for better understanding, for spiritual enlightenment, for growth, for appreciation...

We would already know what is here, there, and yonder.

We would just be—without ever becoming.

We would be as Gods without their minions, creation, through whom and through which They have Their mode of learning...

What if there were no time?

We would live in the present.

But if we are immortal, to which we surely aspire, all things would happen to us at once—in a jumble. We would be born, live, and die, all in the very same moment. We would never linger a whit gazing at a flower, never lean back and wonder at the cloudless blue yonder, nor watch convoluting clouds pile angels and monsters. Never would we dream of far places beyond the timeless ocean. Nor would we ever regard, awed, astonished, starry-eyed the star-light—longing, never sated, unfulfilled desire... pondering the myriad suns suspended in just a single instant, an ephemeral fragment of eternity that isn't.

Nor would we ever witness a child learning his or her first lesson, never stroll a rose garden—his tiny hand in ours... never see him, nor her, grow in wisdom and knowledge—not if there were no time, no sequence to our being...

And yet there's so much beauty, enchantment to last a lifetime... to stretch, in poignant promise to the blurred edges of orderly potential... harmonious and unfolding, infinite seeds of life in the ocean of living, of horizons beguiling, forever receding...

What if there were no God?

There would be no religions. Or would we create our own fickle gods to sate our need for longing? In whose image would you and I come into boundless being?

Yet... if there were no God would flowers still exude their scintillating fragrance? Would the birds still sing songs, hymns of joy, of ebullient pleasure? Would the trees still weave their arms into crowns of such resplendent glory? Would the sun still kiss our face with caring warmth on a summer's morning...? Would we still perceive beauty and harmony and order, or die ignorant and empty, without ever aspiring?

Would you and I still marvel at mystery of awareness? Or would our hearts empty, devoid of God or Goodness, beat hollow, barren measure, till death grants us freedom from senselessness of being?

Or perhaps, hopefully, the universe might not even be there—stars, planets nor moonlight might never have happened... Neither would have you nor I yet risen from the primeval cauldron...

Neither would I be now writing this soliloquy of sorrow.

Nor yet would you, nor any lonesome soul, have lived to read it...

What, say, if instead, we leave things—exactly as we found them?

***

010111

38

CHILDREN

When we finally discover whether it is God who created us, or, perhaps, whether we have created God, we might no longer need to call ourselves children of God. This would in no way deny the existence of God. It would deny, however, the existence of a personified God whose children we have a need of being. Until that moment in our evolution, we shall continue to desire to be looked after, to be nurtured, protected, punished on occasion, rewarded even more often. Indeed, just like children.

Frankly, like *little* children.

I know many people who refuse to give up this childish attachment. God, in whatever form, whatever manifestation we imagine, by whatever act of faith, is not concerned, never was concerned, by all accounts never will be concerned, with us as embodiments of matter and energy. No matter how much we need to create a God in our own image and likeness, quite evidently God refuses to succumb. It seems that His or Her or Its realm is not our physical body, nor our emotions, nor even our mind. No wonder the Christ often repeated that His kingdom is *not* of this world. It is not of this material, emotional or mental world. This unholy triumvirate is ours and our alone. Here, on earth, we are the absolute rulers. We are the kings, sovereign over our domain. Or can be. Here, as the psalmist said so many ears ago, we are gods. Until we cut strings of the Mother Goddess' apron, until we stand up on our own feet, we shall remain children of God. Unfortunately this relationship will forever remain a one way streak.

And it is high time we weaned ourselves away from our imaginary Creator.

Our physical bodies are in a constant state of decay. The presence of Spirit within us galvanizes (the bible calls it "quickens") a continuous cycle of regeneration. The fingers that type this very line will no longer exist by the time this line will have been written. They will have mostly atrophied. New cells, new atoms, new subatomic particles will have replaced the old cells, the old atoms and subatomic particles which constituted my fingers of microseconds ago. The old fingers are dead. As is the rest of me. The old me.

In a way, physically, we are all dead. Spiritually we are reborn. Continuously.

The energy that galvanizes our constituent parts into this cycle of regeneration is called Life. And Life, or Spirit, is an attribute of God.

Our need to create God in our image and likeness is not restricted to religions. We started by worshipping the strongest man in our tribe. The best hunter, the best provider, ultimately the best leader. Later, we sated our needs by paying homage to princes, kings, eventually prime-ministers or presidents. On occasion, the weaker amongst us stooped to pay homage to the miscreants who called themselves great leaders, emperors or Führers.

Concurrently, religions attempted to tear us away from the worship of human or non-human idols. And we, in our childish way, promptly succumbed to the worship of ecclesiastic personages who, wittingly or not, aided us in this endeavor by donning flamboyant robes embroidered with silk and glitter, raised their stature with impressive tall-hats, and generally bedecked themselves in coruscating paraphernalia. They also adopted impressive titles presumably to help us find them worthy objects of our worship. We bowed deeply to them, often bent our knee, kissed their manicured hands and allotted them the entire appropriate if pompous flourish.

Finally, fed up with the broken promises, we stooped even lower.

We began to worship some invisible though almighty figures we carefully constructed to sate our need for being little, irresponsible children. We always attempted to create such invisible beings throughout our history, whenever we have been let down by the lesser gods living among us at our expense.

Now older, putatively more mature, we elevate our gods to rule us from above, from the high heavens. We raise our eyes to the infinite expanse of stars resplendent in our night sky hoping for a miracle. We give those imaginary beings even more impressive titles, we bow to them even lower, we prostrate ourselves and tremble under an imaginary whip, which we expect the objects of our imagination to wield at any moment. To balance the fears generated by our puerile minds, we balance the imaginary beings' thunder with a doze of infinite mercy, with paternal or maternal concern for our scurrilous well-being.

All to remain as children.

In the meantime, our bodies continue to deteriorate, we continue to get sick, to suffer mental, emotional and physical anguish, to go hungry, to die, often in agony, often in the name of an imaginary though almighty being. We all hope to be rewarded for our faithfulness to the figments of our imagination by going to an imaginary heaven, to paradise, where we expect to rest on our fatuous laurels for ever-after.

Whatever happened to the teaching of a Man who once said: "Heaven is within you?" To the teaching of the prophet who said: "Ye are gods?" We ignore their admonitions and decide to be reborn, just once, usually as new-born Christians.

There is no such thing as a new-born Christian.

Every one of us is, I repeat, continuously reborn. All the time. Whether we like it or not. If you are a Christian, you are continuously reborn. If you are Moslem or Hindû or Buddhist or a member of any other religion, you are continuously reborn. What we must decide is what we shall do with this incredible knowledge. How can we co-operate with this Life force, this Spirit, with God—if you must—to extend the potential of this incredible continuous, regenerative, creative, unifying power to the utmost? To be reborn in Spirit is to identify with the Life force, not with the rotting carcass.

It seems that after some more years, perhaps one or two more lifetimes of studying this vital wisdom, this incredible piece of good news, this gospel, we are bound to conclude that co-operation with God means working for common good. It means adopting universal values in place of parochial interests. It has been termed "loving our neighbor" as much as the Infinite Potential ever renewing our state of being. Then we shall begin to act like adults. Until that day, however, we shall continue to cringe in the kindergarten of our own making.

Until that day, we shall remain but children of God.

***

010115

When I was a child,
I spake as a child,
I understood as a child,
I thought as a child:
but when I became a man,
I put away childish things.

Paul
I Corinthians 13:11

39

IMMORTALITY

We mustn't worry about death. In a purely physical sense, we hover on the thin line between living and dying all the time. For some reason, most people call this 'life'. Spiritually, we are indivisible parts of That which is eternal. What is in question is our individuality. As we withdraw our consciousness from our physical bodies, i.e. stop continuously recreating or regenerating our cells, atoms and sub-atomic particles of the body which houses us during the particular period of becoming, our consciousness retains the characteristics which assure its individuality. The traits it developed in a physical body.

That's the good news.

What it means is that the *universal* traits we managed to develop will remain with us as long as the universe lasts. What is less pleasant is that all the other traits which are self-serving, egoistic, mundane if you will (the cause of all our afflictions and sorrows), are ours to be re-absorbed again on our way back to the next stint of becoming.

This is both nice and not so nice.

The nice part is that when we leave our physical bodies (people call this dying), our consciousness (individualized Soul) retains all the characteristics it developed on earth. This means, and this is the nice part, that, providing our loved-ones, the so called dearly-departed, have not as yet constructed and entered another physical sheath (reincarnated), we have a good chance of not only meeting them but actually recognizing them on the "other side". The wives can meet their husbands, the children their parents, and, of course, vice versa. We must never forget that our real body is spiritual, but for the purpose of accelerating our learning, we wrap our spiritual body in sheaths that provide us with sensitivity necessary to experience the process of becoming. These sheaths provide us with the ability to experience emotions, imagination, intellectual appreciation, as well as the five senses of the physical body that we all take for granted. We tend to forget that it took us millions of years to evolve those organs. Anyway, some people call these sheaths astral or imaginative, mental or psychic bodies. The names are unimportant, the knowledge of the process is vital, because we cannot take conscious charge of our lives until we know what instruments we have at our disposal. Until we learn the architecture of our nature, we remain in the reactive stage of evolution, as are all animals, plants and even lower forms of 'life'.

Nevertheless, all this is still in the 'nice' part of the equation.

Unfortunately, once we return for another stint on earth, the problem of recognition becomes very acute. To stop ourselves from going mad, we *temporarily* erase from memory our previous performances (reincarnations). To aid us in this endeavor, we make sure that our new bodies, environments, age groups, and all other interrelationships are completely changed, while retaining all the traits, good and bad, we already developed. There is a very good chance that we shall continue to study the universal truth still in the company of our loved-ones, alas, we are unlikely to recognize them. Your father in the previous 'life' may now be your daughter, your mother your uncle, and that dear sister of yours—a son-in-law. The new arrangements will have been made to maximize learning opportunities for all concerned. There is absolutely no point in repeating the same relationships again, for the simple reason that we would continue to repeat the same mistakes. People are well known for repeating the same peccadilloes *ad infinitum*, or as the formula goes, "till death do us part." We are given a fresh chance in more way than one.

But this only takes us a few reincarnations (lives) forward.

Hardly immortality.

Well, as already mentioned, an individualized Soul is immortal. Just as nothing physical ever disappears in the universe (although the black holes raise an interesting question), nor do non-physical manifestations such as emotions, thoughts or ideas. They linger in the virtual universe ever ready to be re-entered, 'used' for the purpose of learning or just simply enjoyment, and then recycled, as all else is recycled in the world we live in. I find it quite surprising that a number of the, so-called, scientists deny this premise while insisting that only matter and energy have this characteristic. It would be interesting to observe how their children would fare if the 'scientific' fathers and mothers withdrew love from their family equation. The 'materialists' would soon learn what an incredibly powerful energy love is. No matter, they too are immortal, and they too will come to accept the realty as it is.

So it seem evident that you and I have no beginning, no end.

This is what being immortal means.

Theoretically, once an individualized Soul acquires conscious control over all the universal values, it has an option to merge or be re-absorbed into the Singularity of Being. This Singularity, the Oneness, we call God. We have already established that Life as an attribute of God is by definition eternal. There is, however, a catch. The problem is that this 're-absorption', as some Buddhists call it, might never happen. God, again by definition, is infinite in all perfections. In other words, we could only acquire the infinite divine traits in the infinity of time. Only infinity is an ever-receding horizon. A billion billion-billion years from now we shall experience the first day, the first hour, and the first second, of "the rest" of our existence. The same will happen a further billion billion-billion years down the road. Infinity refuses to accept limitations.

This is what makes God—God.

It seems that we are stuck in the eternal process of becoming.

You will forever be you, even as I shall remain I. (Ouch?)

We might not like it, but we can only become God when we can do all the things God does. As my teacher of some years ago said, the only way to be Master is to act like a Master. I have a long way to go. Perhaps—an infinity of becoming. The more I learn the more there will be to learn.

Isn't Life fun?

The sooner we fully accept the constituents of our true nature, the sooner we shall embark on our *conscious* journey. From that moment on we shall learn from everyone, but we shall no longer follow in anyone's footsteps. Each one of us will be able to say, "I am the way."

As indeed, each of us—Is.

***

010116

The heavenly is like Tao. Tao is the Eternal.
The decay of the body is not to be feared.

Lao-tse
Lao-tse, TAO TEH KING, 16.
[Translation by Dwight Goddard,
Lao tzu's Tao and Wu Wei. New York, 1919]

40

THE FUTURE

Attempting to decipher the various scriptures is a little like trying to solve the New York Times crossword puzzle without knowing the English language. And in the case of scriptures there are many languages, all of them ancient, dead, not used for thousands of years. Perhaps that is why the scriptures limited themselves to the predictions affecting individual people, to the evolution of an individual soul or consciousness, rather than to paint, even in broadest strokes, the material environs in which this soul will enjoy its becoming. The material vision is left to little us, the stumbling, erring, vagabonds of the physical reality.[1]

Yet neither religions nor science deny that there is a future lurking behind, or rather in front of, the future millennia. There, ready and waiting, the future is laying out playing fields for our imagination to conquer, new horizons to reach for, new secrets to uncover.

I always found it fascinating how members of my species (this includes some of my best friends), the Homo-reputedly-sapiens, managed to imagine that, while there is indisputable evidence that in our immediate vicinity we affect the course of nature's unfolding, "out there", beyond the last horizons, things "just happen." Perhaps controlled by immutable laws of the universe, but nevertheless, not being the result of anyone's will, of anyone's desires or even blunders.

Look at it this way.

A billion-billion-billion years from now, we shall all be still around, only we shall, of course, be awfully nice. Saints if you will. I don't mean in the tedious sense of clasping our hands together and staring into the infinity of space, or at some extraordinarily beautiful picture of another saint, but we shall manifest a great assortment of universal traits. We shall be many times more powerful in relation to man of today, than we now are in relation to most other species on earth. By today's standards, our science will be like magic. We shall probably govern some great planets, perhaps planetary systems. I don't mean as people govern segments of earth, but we shall be the "powers-behind-the-throne." The smarter among us will probably administer minor galaxies. I say minor, because the Hobble telescope recently showed us two major galaxies that bumped into each other about 100 million years ago. Someone boobed. And an error like that spans some 20,000 light years of intergalactic space.[2] My advice for the future: stick to minor galaxies.

We shall commune with each other by extra sensory perception, only the perception will not be anything extra but rather run of the mill. Should we want to, we shall teleport ourselves for a *tête-à-tête* with our nearest universal relative, who will probably be able to meet us half way, in whatever form, appearance, or manner we both desire. There will be no question of the velocity-of-light limitation, because we shall have learned to convert our constituent parts into zero-mass quanta, and reassemble them on a moment's notice by an act of our will. Or just reconstitute ourselves, in a different place, from the available materials. If we feel too tired to do that, we shall remain where we are, and merely contract or expand space itself. There are no restrictions on this technique in any theory I've ever heard of.
Could be rather fun.

Difficult? Unlikely?
Look what we've done in just a few thousand years of civilization. Sure we are still stupid and primitive, and... well,

never mind; but we, as a species, did produce Michelangelo, Leonardo da Vinci, Mozart, Einstein, Socrates, not to mention a number of extraordinarily advanced souls we know as Avatars.

Just think what we can do in a billion-billion-billion years!

Isn't it a good thing we're immortal? And we can keep trying, as my local priest likes to say, for ever-and-ever. Only the padre refers to something else. But that too will change. There is plenty of time.

The adherents of various religions have told us that, after death, we shall meet in heaven, and/or on different planets, both material and spiritual. (I refuse to discuss the more unpleasant alternatives). The first is the favorite haunt of the Christians, the second apparently frequented by the Hindûs. Both, I feel, are right and both are wrong. There may well be planes at which we perceive and experience reality in quite different fashion to our present intimacy. But I would hesitate to accept, on faith, any concept that limits anything, in any way, whatsoever. If we accept that God is infinite, then we cannot put limits on the development of our perception. And we must never forget that God has no being other than in a mode of being.

As discussed in my previous essay, Life is neither past nor future but One, continuous, eternal condition of becoming. We shall never lose our individuality, but we shall lose our parochial views. As Peter once said: "Of a truth, I perceive that God is no respecter of persons."[3] Essentially, on our endless journey of becoming, we shall grow more and more similar to each other. Call it Spiritual entropy. It will bring us much closer together. Often, at will, we shall be able to *feel* as one. But in the early stages of our spiritual development, we shall carry our physical, emotional and mental traits for many generations.

Perhaps, a few billion years...

There is a magnificent difference between the future as defined by our earthly clocks, and the future as seen through spiritual eyes. One leads to dilapidation of our physical bodies, deterioration of our senses, to all the proclivities of aging and the attendant maladies, to a growing condition of being tired...
The other is bursting with energy, with ever growing joy of recognition of our infinite potential. It is bursting with an ever-growing awareness of our immortality—of living in constant awe of the indescribable beauty still lying before us.

***

010116

FOOTNOTES

(1). By 'soul' with a small 's', I am referring to individualization the One Soul.
(2). I am referring to the collision between the galaxy NGC 1410 and NGC 1409.
(3). Acts of the Apostles 10:34

The man of science is a poor philosopher

Albert Einstein

41

MASTERS AND MINIONS

Most of us aspire to great successes. To fame and riches, to ascendancy over others, be it through physical, emotional, intellectual, or mental powers. We want to leave our mark, stake our claim, gain recognition and—hopefully—admiration. This is because, for the most part, we are still minions.

There is a good reason why so many of us cannot understand the medial path advocated by the great Avatars. Whether we call it the Straight and Narrow, the Middle Path of Buddha, or the esoteric Tao, it all comes to the same thing. Yet most of us needn't worry. Middle Path is reserved for aspiring Masters. Minions are of little consequence.

The minions are already taken care of.

The minions, the average Joe or Mary, have so little knowledge (which translates into power), so puny is their influence over their environment that their feelings, attitudes or actions are unlikely to cause any noticeable harm nor to benefit an appreciable number of people. Not so with the Masters. Those who find the "key to the kingdom" wield such enormous authority that its misuse can destroy individuals on contact, and, what is worse, affect adversely the welfare of very great numbers. Hitler, Stalin, earlier Napoleon or Genghis Hun held partial keys to this power. Great leaders all. Certainly more than minions. Yet great many corpses, great suffering, lay in their grotesque shadows—silent witnesses to the horrendous abuse of power.

Luckily, those with truly great knowledge seldom rise to exercise it.

Men endowed with the ability to perform 'miracles' never allowed themselves to wield power over others. Should they choose to do so, the minions would be unable to resist. The true Masters invariably affirm that all power resides within each one of us, and that this power is one and identical with that which is within themselves. Others, awed by the secrets of the past Masters, organize religions, churches, in an attempt to arrogate some of this mysterious power. Yet, for the most part, such men are little more than self-serving minion. They invariably fail. Even Paul of Tarsus, undoubtedly a Master, crossed the danger line by attempting to cast pearls before swine. This is why, during the last 1500 years or so, few Masters have made their presence known. They choose to remain in the shadows, maintain a "low profile", and seldom if ever teach. There is always danger someone would create a religion out of his or her teaching, a full-proof method of subjugating minions. And, after all, knowledge is already available to all that seek it.

There is another reason why the Middle Path is so strongly advocated.

As we rise through the rungs of wisdom, we begin to wonder in the corridors of real might. Within these hallowed halls, there are no signposts leading to good or evil. The gift of freewill is not withdrawn. All our potential, for both, good and evil, remains with us, or rather within us. There, we can as easily move mountains to open new horizons, as to drop them on the unsuspecting heads of recalcitrant minions. The story of the Archangel Lucifer gives us a fair warning. The higher we rise in knowledge, the greater the temptation of abuse. I've already listed some dire examples.

The danger *never* abates.

So what is the way out?

According to the Masters, there are two safety valves. First, we must never stray from the middle ground. The Creative Power, ever available in the mysterious realm of virtual reality, admittedly manifests bias towards the positive spectrum. But It doesn't impose Itself. This is, we might say, the curse of free-will. The power will flow to anyone able to use It. For good *and* for evil.

The second safety valve is the oft-repeated counsel to love one-another. This admonition, properly understood, erases the distinction between you and me, between us and them. It is the rationale behind the golden rule.[1] In the ultimate sense, love is that which opens our eyes to the Truth that, at the ground of our being, we are all One.

Those content to remain minions, are in relatively little danger. Jesus called such people the 'dead', the (as yet) "not alive" to their true potential.[2] Krishna speaking to Arjuna says: "...the ignorant perform their duties with attachment to results... let not the wise disrupt the minds of the ignorant who are attached to fruitive action."[3] But Jesus warns that we must also be sure not to judge others.[4] Paul Twitchell once said that a sure way to know that we are not yet Masters is to think ourselves better than others.

And, after all, the higher we rise, the deeper the menacing chasm.

Yet the various world religions continue to make the same mistake. There is a difference between casting pearls before swine, and telling 'swine' that pearls do not exist. All too often the organized religions offer half-truths which serve to maintain the state of abject ignorance, thus making their followers amenable to exploitation. To say less or even nothing is better than to create an unnatural barrier between man and his ultimate potential.[5]

Nevertheless, all messages, instructions, knowledge, inspiration, of the Avatars of yore had been meant always, invariably, and *exclusively* for the aspiring Masters. This knowledge has never been intended for the minions, the masses. The minions have been studiously ignored. There was neither disrespect, nor humbling, nor downgrading in this stance, but merely full awareness that the inner knowledge is as incomprehensible to all who are not awakened to the spiritual reality. Rather as quantum physics are to a man or woman who can neither read nor write. We must never forget that every single minion *retains the potential* of opening him/herself to the inner knowledge, to become gods in waiting. The will, the commitment, the single eye—is missing. Without single-mindedness there cannot be any results. And until the minions awaken to these facts, none of this makes any sense to them. They will continue to live under the inexorable laws of nature with the rest of flora and fauna.

Such is material reality.

Thus, at the early stages of evolution we are in a reactive mode of being, reacting to hardships and boons bobbing our ships on the dull, stagnant, uninspired waters. At this stage, ignorance is bliss—or what substitutes for bliss. But for those already awakened, those who dared to reach out for the tiller, I offer just those two admonitions: the middle path and the love of one's neighbor. These alone *guarantee* to save us from dire consequences of our erroneous actions. At the beginning, as the saying goes, little knowledge is a dangerous thing. And we all start at the bottom.

Those who are Masters-in-waiting, those awakened to their true nature of being, realize that the attributes of God are the attributes available to each one us. There is a difference, of course, between availability and gaining ability to use them.

The latter is what life is all about.

***

01011

FOOTNOTES

(1). "Do unto others as you would have them do unto you."

(2). "Let the dead bury their dead." Matthew 8:22.

(3). Bhagavad-Gita 3:25-26 [The Bhaktivedanta Book Trust, Los Angeles, 1972]

(4). Luke 6:37

(5). Compare Luke 11:52

42

RECUMBENT EVOLUTION

One of the greatest artists has done us irreparable harm. No matter how much we deny it, Michelangelo's Father image, so brilliantly depicted on the ceiling of the Sistine chapel, etched in indelible mark on our minds. No matter how much we deny it, during any discussion, sooner of later, we shall detect some connotations of a long flowing beard, of powerful yet kindly face ever ready to punish and reward us with full measure of divine justice. Perhaps, for a time, it was meant to be so.

But as our communication skills have broadened, we grew less ignorant. Our Internet, TV and radio daily flood our eyes, ears and minds with reports of cataclysmic earthquakes, volcanic eruptions, of destructive flooding or tsunami, elsewhere of arid spells resulting in ongoing suffering—yes, suffering of little children. When we witness His silent acquiescence in wars, in mass-murders, in horrors of unimaginable scope and variety, the Fatherly image seems to lose some of Its luster. If there be power controlling our daily struggle, then it is hardly a benevolent power, or, at the very least, a power quite singularly indifferent to our fate.

People pray for deliverance to the figments of their imagination. God is no longer plastered on the ceiling of Sistine chapel, nor keeping council in gilt tabernacles, nor in mosques ornate with arabesque profusion, nor in any other temple. We must look for Him much closer. Perhaps as close as the silent whisper in the stillness of our hearts.

There, at least, we might find serene, divine solace.

Perhaps it is time to really revise the image of God we carry in our childish delusions. Not just to pay lip service to a more 'adult' vision of a Divine Being, but to drop, once and for all, the image of Paternal Protection. It has been proven a million times over, that the Father of us all, the Creative Principle no longer regards us as little children in need of a grownup's protection. Or we might even go as far as accepting the teaching of Jesus who claimed, repeatedly, that his Father's concerns are *not* of this world. That here we are on our own, in this valley of abundant tears. His apostles repeated that here, as we saw so shall we reap.[1] We might as well go a step further, and, as far as this world is concerned, erase the Fatherly figure altogether, and realize, once and for all, that the tears, in this lachrymose valley, are self-induced, self-propagated, and invariably self-inflicted. That this world has been long set on automatic, and the sooner we learn how it works, the sooner we shall wipe dry the tears with our knowledge, understanding and sense of responsibility.

In spirit, we are immortal, but that's of little comfort to one hungry or thirsty, and having no knowledge how to procure food for one's children. For that we must rely on evolution, on our evolutionary skills, and those, quite unwittingly, we have brought to a sudden stop.

That's right.

We, the dominant species of the mother earth, brought our own evolution to an untimely demise. We stopped evolving. We are standing still. Perhaps regressing. And most of us haven't even noticed.

There is only one way that an ameba could have evolved to become a human being. One way only that the amino acids combined their helix structures to bring us to where we are now. And that was through two factors, one—natural selection, and two—lucky errors. Yes, errors. If nature were left to her own, we would have started treading water thousands of years ago. Only the cataclysms we despise so much caused us to look elsewhere for our salvation than in the compulsive maintenance of the same arrangement of genes. Only untoward slips in the natural clockworks enabled us to take tiny steps on the upward facing ladder.

And now, we have stopped it.

Rather than improve our bodies, our physiques, our immune systems, our internal and external biological abilities, we have learned more and more how to control our climate. There is no reason for us to learn to overcome excessive heat with the air-conditioner whirling at a nearby windowsill. There is no reason to teach our bodies to withstand vicious drops in temperature, if we can switch on the electric heater. Nor do we need to improve our immune system when we can eat tons of antibiotics, sera and other concoctions that serve to render us helpless without them. We need not concentrate on breading the best, the healthiest, when nature's own discards are maintained in incubators until just fit enough to lower the average health of our species. Those weaker genes, lacking perhaps in mental or physical prerogatives conducive to survival, shall be perpetrated by "God given" right to bread litter in our own image and likeness.

And, the amazing thing is that we are doing all this in the name of love. Love of my own rights, my own needs, my own selfishness, my own dignity. Never, *never*, for the good of others. What would, one can but wander, say the Fatherly image on the Sistine chapel to such a choice of action?

And yet the only people who attempt to improve the evolutionary stock of our species appear, or are judged, to be deviants. We condemn out-of-hand the dreams of a Super Race, of the Nietzchean *Ubermensch*, just because such aspirations are invariably advocated by pretenders hungry for world domination. We are the gentle people. We examine our animals if they are sufficiently healthy to be slaughtered, but we do our best to maintain our own progeny alive and unwell for as long as possible. There is some twisted logic in this sort of behavior, but it is at odds with the laws of nature.

Perhaps the first steps we should take are to feed all people, regardless of race or convictions, then teach them how to look after themselves, before we concentrate so much on adding billions of 'souls' to our, as yet, unbalanced economy. A week spent in Calcutta will cure anyone from the Western ambition to add hungry mouths at the expense of others. Then we might allow our doctors, through the miracles of modern medicine, to decide on the viability of the fetuses, *before* they are quickened by the presence of Soul. We might finally listen to the great mystics telling us that Consciousness invades the new-born child's body with the first breath.

With the first *pneuma*, a Greek word which also means Spirit.

Perhaps we should let God's be what is God's, and Caesar's what is Caesar's, and provide Soul with the very best vehicles *we* possibly can, to let It fill our lives with meaning. As Soul we are immortal, but as physical body endowed with mind and imagination we, and we alone, are responsible for our earthly wellbeing. And every time we forget this, we shall once more fill this beautiful valley with tears.

***

010116

FOOTNOTES

(1). Galatians 5:7 et al.

A man came to Rumi and said, "Please God that I could go to the other world; there at least I could be at peace because the Creator is there."

"What do you know about where He is?" answered Rumi. "Everything in all the worlds is in you; whatever you are hungering for, work for it here by yourself, for you are the microcosm."

Jalal-ud-Din Rumi
Harvey, Andrew, LIGHT UPON LIGHT,
Inspirations from RUMI
[North Atlantic Books, Berkeley, California 1996; p.53]

43

ALL PLEASURE

Rereading (yet again) the heavily edited copy of Bhagavad-Gita I came across a fascinating item I'd missed before. According to the translator and commentator of the scripture, Srila Prabhupâda, the literal translation of Sanskrit word *Krishna* is "all pleasure". Since to the Hindûs the name Krishna represents "the Supreme Lord" or the absolute Divinity, it is truly a wonderful appellation. 'Krishna', writes Srila Prabhupâda, "is the reservoir of pleasure. Our consciousness seeks happiness because we are part and parcel of the Lord." And then he adds an absorbing thought: "...if we dovetail our activities with His, we will partake of His happiness."

Quite a proposition.

Imagine if our Christian images weren't connected or associated with the cross and suffering. Imagine the mood of all Christians if their worship was directed towards a Being (yes, most Hindûs personify their God even as Christians do) Who in the ultimate sense fills our minds and hearts with All Pleasure.

A truly wondrous idea.

Whenever we pray, we would think of Pleasure. We wouldn't go to church to gaze at a body of an innocent Man nailed to a cross, but we would bathe our senses in an esoteric, perhaps all encompassing joy. Yet, safe for some circumspect masochists of the Christian religions, does this Far Eastern concept differ so much from the *original* teaching of Christ? I recall an assurance from the First Apocalypse of James: *The Lord said, "James, do not be concerned for me... I am he who was within me. Never have I suffered in any way, nor have I been distressed."*[1]

By contrast, I do find it distressing indeed that Christians who assign divine powers to the Lord, to Christ, imagine that He could not or would not have dismissed all mental, emotional, not to mention physical, pain or anguish. There are many people who can, by an act of their will, switch off the awareness of *any* discomfort. Yet the Lord could not? Surely the faithful do not imagine that He was a willing participant in this very human weakness. That would be paramount to masochism.

In their introduction to the Gospel of Truth, Attridge and MacRae point out that the revelation of the gospel results in a state of wakefulness *"...a condition of joy and delight graphically contrasted with the nightmarish existence of those in ignorance."*[2] And then, as pointed out by Professor Pagels in the Acts of John, we are told: *"I have suffered none of the things which they will say of me; even that suffering which I showed to you and to the rest of my dance, I will that it be called a mystery."*[3] Finally, if we are still not convinced, there is this seemingly enigmatic statement: *"Learn how to suffer and you shall be able not to suffer."*[4]

Yet people, particularly the Christians, think that by suffering they are emulating their Master. The Master who, according to the Bhagavad-Gita, the Gnostic gospels and the Apocrypha quoted, appears to be "all pleasure." Could so many scriptures be wrong? There must have been a reason why all such references have been carefully removed, surgically excised, from the orthodox version of the Christian scriptures. What would the churches do if all their faithful learned not to suffer? To be full of joy? After all, the New Testament shows ample evidence of being filled with "all pleasure". "I bring you good tiding of *great joy*" writes

Luke.[5] "These things write we to you, *that your joy may be full,*" echoes John.[6] There are *many* other references.
What happened?
Where is this abundant joy in the eyes, faces, in the hearts of the Christians I see? Why is there such preponderance of suffering in the images displayed throughout all the churches I've ever visited? Oh, I am sure there are exceptions, there always are. But the vast majority? Whose idea was it to change the purpose, the main thrust, of Christ's teaching? For what reason?

All Pleasure.
A truly fitting title to a Deity I could well believe in. In fact I do. I am surrounded with Pleasure. Sometimes I slip into the characteristic mood pervading the atmosphere around me, but... seldom. Of late, almost never. How could we possibly not be joyful when we were given implicit instructions how to achieve unshakeable joy? Uninterrupted pleasure? Abundant peace? Wealth beyond our wildest dreams? Eternity of joyful discovery? Ever receding horizons? And there is more... infinitely more...
And all we have to do is to study the wisdom of the ages. Not the twisted, distorted versions of those who wish to tell us what is 'really' in the secret texts. What the texts 'really' mean. Not the second hand raving all those who wish to impose their misbegotten views of the necessity of suffering. Not the diluted versions but the originals, or as close to the originals as we can get. Trust me, there is enough Truth left in all of them. Even though Buddha, in his four noble truths, acknowledges the existence of suffering, he also tells us how to *stop* suffering. And it isn't so difficult.
All we must do is knock.
The doors will, surely, be opened.

***
010120

FOOTNOTES

(1). THE NAG HAMMADI LIBRARY IN ENGLISH, James M. Robinson, General Editor. [HarperSanFrancisco1978] THE FIRST APOCALYPSE OF JAMES, p.265.
(2). ibid, THE GOSPEL OF TRUTH, introduced and translated by Harold W. Attridge and George W. MacRae, p.39.
(3). Pagels, Elaine THE GNOSTIC GOSPELS, [Vintage Books, Div. of Random House, New York, 1981; pg. 89-90]. From NEW TESTAMENT APOCRYPHA, ACTS OF JOHN. (transl. from *Neutestamentliche Apocryphen*, Philadelphia 1963]
(4). ibid. ACTS OF JOHN
(5). Luke 2:10
(6). The First Epistle Gen. of John 1:4

The optimist fell ten stories.
At each window bar he shouted to his friends:

"All right so far."

Unknown

44

OXYMORONS AND MISNOMERS

At first sight, oxy- has something to do with oxygen and moron with ah, well... with a moron. In fact, oxy- shares it's acerbic taste with a mode of expression coming from Greek *oxys* meaning sharp, acid. The moron component corresponds rather well to people who use this literary form unwittingly, deriving its root once again from the Greek's *moros*, meaning dull, foolish, as in *ingeniously stupid*, but also as in *thunderous silence* or, as Shakespeare put it, "parting is such *sweet sorrow*". Thus oxymoron is an expression, which at first sight at least, appears rather sharp though... foolish. Some oxymorons, however, seem to persist in the foolishness while loosing their acuity.

Misnomer is much simpler to define. Should anyone have any doubts, it refers to the act of applying a wrong name or epithet to a person or thing. Sometimes it is hard to decide, however, which term applies better: *oxymoron* or a *misnomer*.

The word 'catholic' comes to mind. 'Catholic', as Noah Webster will attest, means universal, general, again from splitting the *katholikos* into *kata* meaning down, and *holos* whole. The Concise Oxford Dictionary defines the meaning of the word as follows: universal, *of interest or use to all men; all-embracing, of wide sympathies, broadminded, tolerant.*

Now this is when the acerbic-foolishness creeps in. Since the word 'catholic' has been appropriated by the Roman Church, it, the word not the church, became embroiled in such oxymoronic filigree as to misrepresent the very fundamentals of the Church. I think it is safe to say that the Church that calls itself Roman-Catholic never was, isn't, and shows no signs of having the slightest intention of becoming 'catholic'.

Let me count the ways...

An organization that claims to control the faith of barely one-sixth of the populations of the world (and proportionately shrinking) is not *universal*. Further, the Catholic Church was never *all-embracing*. In fact it was as standoffish as any organization can be. It assured all its opponents that unless they join them, they would fry in hell for an indeterminate but assuredly extremely long period of time. *Exclusionary* would be a better word.

Next let us deal with *broadminded*. How can anyone claim to be broadminded when one declares all who disagree with one a heretic? This very appellation imposed by the Church attests to the oxymoronic (i.e.: acerbic and foolish) application of the word 'catholic'. Heretic comes (yes, again the Greeks...) from *hairetikos* meaning *able to choose*. Now, if the heretics are by definition able to choose, then, surely, the members of the 'Catholic' church are not, which brings me to the penultimate meaning of the word 'catholic: *tolerant*. Now here the oxymoron lost even a pretence of an *oxy-* and sunk into the depth of the *moros*. One simply isn't tolerant when one refuses, on principle, to allow any choice.

Oxymorons galore? Or just a screaming misnomer?

Now let us for a moment look at the heretics. They enjoy *freedom-of-choice*, thus they are, by definition, *tolerant* of others, they are certainly of *wide-sympathies*. And since there are, in the eyes of the Roman Church five heretics to every 'catholic', then we could safely say that the heretics are fairly *all-embracing*. Almost *universal*.

Yes, the heretics are definitely catholic. The only Catholics.

Why is it that such a vivid misnomer, or be it oxymoron, is so important to an organization which, in so many other areas can and does so much good? Perhaps if the Church had another couple of popes like John XXIII or the present John-

Paul II, the pomposity of meaningless titles would be gradually eradicated. Alas, J-P II is 80 and ailing, and I'm sure he has more important things on his mind than lecturing his *Curia Romana* on etymology.

Yet, such are the corridors of power.

And talking of power brings to mind the Queen of England.

Here, we find an amazing oxymoron *in reverse*.

Misnomer, if you insist.

The illustrious 'Queen' has many ancillary meanings. There is queen-conch, queen-craft, queen-fish, queen-gold, also queen-lily, -consort, -dowager, -counsel and queen-cake. Enough said, there are queens galore. The word Queen, usually with a capital 'Q', is understood to mean a monarch or a ruler. The Queen of *England*, also carries the titles of *"Elizabeth the Second, by the Grace of God, of the United Kingdom of Great Britain and Northern Island, and Her other Realms and Territories Queen, Head of the Commonwealth, Defender of the Faith."* Now, I have no intention of questioning Her Majesty's affectionate authority over her minions, but really, since the barons forced King John to sign the *Magna Carta* in 1215, all kings and queens became more like lame ducklings than monarchs, Grace of God notwithstanding. Our present gracious Queen E. II is indeed gracious, nice, reputedly pleasant and even speaks some French. And no! She definitely does not resemble the transatlantic luxury ship.

A monarch, head or defender—she is not.

But this is not the point.

As I mentioned, the word queen is a potential oxymoron *in reverse*. Rather than attempting to live up to the name and title which indeed could be taken as parody of her position, the Queen E., unwittingly or not, reverted to the original meaning of 'queen', thus eliminating both acerbic and foolish connotations. Queen, *quen* in Middle English, and *cwen* in Anglo-Saxon, means, quite simply and univocally... a woman. *A wife and a woman.*

So you see, the Queen is no more an oxymoron. She reverted to being... just a woman, which makes her a queen. Even as my wife is my queen.

So much for oxymorons attendant to the corridors of power.

However, there are other linguistic peccadilloes.

Like people imagining that a *polit*ician has something to do with *polit*eness. The word *policy*, with the appendage *ician*, combine to form *politician*. Now the word policy comes from (you guessed it) Greek *polis*, meaning a city, *not* from Latin *politus* meaning polite. It is true that politicians can be polite when they want your vote, but that's about the end of it. Confusing the root of the word politician with politeness (a sort of univocal polite-politician) is an oxymoron in the making, with the accent on *moros*.

Why all these stories?

To make sure that you don't believe everything you hear. And I don't want you to think that I'm picky. I am quite prepared to show flexibility. As with the word *polish*, meaning *smooth, refined*. Which is just as it should be. Everyone knows that polish must have been originally written with a capital P.

And that's no oxymoron.

***

01012

My religion consists of humble admiration
of the illimitable superior spirit
who reveals himself
in the slight details we are able to perceive
with our frail and feeble mind.

Albert Einstein
[From an Internet collection by Kevin Harris 1995]

45

COWORKERS

Over the years, I have written a numbers of essays in which I discussed various aspects of evolution. I divided them into morsels short enough not to bore the reader and, hopefully, appetizing enough to whet his or her appetite for further reading. But when all is said and done, and written, one aspect of evolution remains paramount. For all who refuse to accept limitations imposed on us by various governments, religions, or other organizations, which derive their power from an acute imposition of conventions, customs, or other established or legislative instruments, we must, sooner or later, face the final challenge. We must shirk the past and face the future unfettered by primitive assumptions. When we achieve this step, we shall finally become Co-workers with the Infinite Potential welling within our Consciousness.

We shall become Coworkers with God.

This step has nothing to do with any religion, any tradition nor any established way. All traditional systems practiced by mankind heretofore are concerned with the *protection* of the human genome. The human gene. We shall throw off the mindset imposed on us by the established (legal, ethical and social) powers bent on the careful manipulation of facts to maintain *status quo*. We shall look outwards. We shall refuse to be fed claptrap in the name of traditions. Darryl Reanney, the distinguished molecular biologist internationally known for his work on the origins of life, writes: "...individuals, living and working within familiar, habitual boundary conditions, are largely unaware of perhaps 80 percent or more of what goes on around them."[1] Most of us live and work within familiar, habitual boundary conditions. Most of us are 80% or more ignorant of whatever is going on outside our social, cultural, professional and mental ghetto.

Such conditions are indeed beneficial for the protection of the human gene. But the absurdity of the situation becomes apparent when this *modus vivendi* actually stalls the natural evolution of the very gene the system we have adopted is bent on protecting. The forward looking scientists, the very few whose feet are not held, knee deep, in the quagmire of yesterday's knowledge masking their pitiful ignorance, are finally, for the first time in the recorded history, able to take conscious part in the evolution of the human gene. In my recent essay *Recumbent Evolution*, I endeavored to demonstrate the brakes, which the philosophical and/or theological attitudes and conditioning imposes on the evolution of human thought. Here, I wish to discuss some aspects of the biological consequences.

As mentioned, we can finally take active part in the Conscious Evolution of our species. We no longer have to wait for a meteor to upset the ecological balance, nor for plagues or other misfortunes to force our genes to take fresh and unfamiliar defensive actions (haphazard mutations). It has been firmly established that the human gene will not evolve one whit when not forced to do so by external conditions. Within well defined limits, it will remain in the condition, (state, mode, posture, molecular structure) nature found most propitious to maintaining *status quo*, and in this mode it will be meticulously maintained even as by our pseudo-theological and political cognoscenti. I say pseudo-theological, because people who talk about God by closing their eyes remain blind to God's work. God and His (Her or

Its) will is abundantly visible all around us. I am not suggesting that God *is* nature, but that nature in which we find our being, Infinite Intelligence is explicitly and implicitly demonstrated. Furthermore, by observing nature we can learn more about this Intelligence and Its divine plan than by countless hours of detached meditation, regular trips to a temple or church, or by faithful allegiance to organizations which bar progress under the penalty of anathema.[2]

I know it is hard to believe but both the reigning pope and the recent president of the United States have spoken boldly against cloning. Yet, the same rulers are more than willing to butcher the members of other species to sustain or extend their own life. Other decadent 'aristocrats' derive pleasure from killing. Just for fun. If our gene is to be superior to other genes, then perhaps we should attempt to breed a race that respects the wellbeing of other species. It is profusely evident that neither legal, social nor ethical authorities have any intention whatever to suggest such a course to their followers.

Yet such a gene may well be possible.

Those among us who cannot, for whatever reason (as yet?), partake in Conscious Evolution, let us at least support the few who try. Who knows, perhaps they will breed a gene that will limit our reproductive efficacy to one or two offspring. Perhaps they will learn to synthesize food so that we do not have to slaughter millions of other species to sustain our own biological (not to mention gluttonous) needs. Perhaps they will strengthen our immune system so that we shall no longer have to pollute nature with billions of tons of chemicals we use to 'improve' our resistance to viruses and bacteria in the creation and evolution of which we have probably, unwittingly, participated.

Let us stop thinking of the past.

Let us stop supporting organizations that are bent on maintaining the decadent policies of yore. The policies of scaremongers promulgating fear of tomorrow in order to protect whatever they have secreted in their ivory towers. We are facing a quite different danger. If we continue to resist evolution, and we do, nature will not be denied. The consequences will not be pleasant. Look at the dinosaurs.

Let us imagine a future in which the concrete jungle reverts to what Nature's intention appears to have been: a Garden of Eden. Let us participate in the creation of a future wherein we can breathe clean air and feel high, drank, on the scent of flowers. This sentiment is not against progress. Just the opposite. It is for the progress of our own selves, not *just* of our gadgets.

I dare say, none of what I've written above is new. The Truth is never new. It has neither beginning nor end. The Truth IS. Just like God. Just like His divine presence within you and me. We can finally stand tall and say *no* to the ignorant past. We can stop being afraid of tomorrow, of death, of hell, of the wrath of God. A few billion years ago, the earth had been no more than an ocean of atoms. Look how far evolution has taken us since. Think how far we can go by participating rather than opposing its progress. How much faster. Think what fun we shall have. We can discover our true potential through the magic of conscious participation in the Creative Process. In Conscious Evolution.

We can finally become Coworkers of God.

***

010123

FOOTNOTES

(1). Reanney, Darryl AFTER DEATH [Avon Books, New York 1991] p.129.

(2). I greatly support meditation, but as a means to enhance life, not as a substitute for it.

46

WEALTH

You cannot give what you haven't got.
Once upon a time, Peter and John, the apostles, came across a beggar lame from birth. The poor man could neither stand nor walk. The two apostles commiserated with the beggar that they had neither silver nor gold to aid him, but they would give him such as they had. "In the name of Jesus Christ of Nazareth rise up and walk," said Peter. And the man did.[1]

I've recounted this story not to describe a miracle, but to illustrate that even if our pockets are quite empty, we can still be wealthy enough to help others. Emmet Fox defines wealth as a state of consciousness. As indeed, everything is. Our consciousness uses the mind to manufacture everything that makes up our reality.

Wealth is achieved by the conversion of Spirit into anything we want. In other words, all it takes is to reach into the Infinite Potential extant within the Virtual Universe and bring it into manifestation as an emotion, an idea or a solid object. This is the way to amass wealth without doing so at anyone's expense. This 'secret' formula has been proposed and advocated by sages of old, and since people of their day would have been unable to understand the concept expressed in 'modern' language, the various elements have been personified (endowed with super-human forms).

Thus heaven and the intelligence inherent to the Field of Infinite Potential have been personified (as was fitting in a culture descendant from Greek influence) as the heavenly Father. It is, after all, a fairly accurate description, since the source, or that, which produces anything, can well be described as the father or progenitor of that particular idea or creation. The inspired *ideas* have been called Angels, or the messengers of God. Various functions of our Higher Self have been referred to as divine intervention. Likewise, the methods of the creative process had been described in many forms, some dating back to the very first chapter of the Genesis.[2] The process itself has been substantially revised and simplified by the man on whose teaching Paul of Taurus organized a new religion which later became known as Christianity. Jesus did his best to assure his followers that "if ye shall ask any thing in my name, I will do it."[3] In *my name* means in *my nature*; and his nature was, of course, spiritual— and spiritual in this context means *beyond any limitations*. The 'I' in the equation is the "Son of God" extant in everyone of us as our Higher Self.[4] If one accepts limitations, *any* limitations, then limitations become manifest in one's life. For the last two thousand years most people lived in abject disappointment. They have not learned to 'ask' correctly. Once learned, however, the formula cannot fail, as has been proven by many people who never heard of Christ's teaching, nor practiced any aspect of the religion instituted by Paul.

The method is *not* a religious doctrine.

It is an aspect of reality we all live in.

To apply the formula correctly, we must understand that everything we might want *already exists within the virtual universe*. To bring it out "into the open", to give it reality in the material universe, we must fulfill a number of steps. Before starting, we must define precisely what it is that we want. We must make absolutely sure that we really want it with all the appurtenances that the new element in our life will carry or entail, and finally, we must never attempt to direct the Process itself with our will or mind. The process itself takes place within the "no-man's land" on the verge of the Virtual Universe. To attempt to control it would be like trying to control the behavior of matter hovering at the event-horizon of a black hole.[5] Anyway, the process is set up to be fail-proof.

Any deviation from these postulates, however, results in failure.

Finally, we must never impose a time factor for the results to be manifest. Some people, for instance, take years to develop an incapacitating disease (by continually breaking universal laws), and then they expect to be healed by the power of a momentary prayer. It may happen, of course, to adepts at the technique. But adepts at the technique would never spend years developing an incapacitating disease. We must leave the time factor to the laws prevalent in the Virtual Universe (the Father or Heaven). And, for the most part, these laws are, as yet, unknown to us. Perhaps this is as it should be, lest we abuse them also. A few other items:

What we cannot do is to ask for that which contravenes Universal Laws.

In matters of the creation of reality, ignorance is not bliss.

Heaven is for the brave, the daring, and the persistent.

In my book *VISUALIZATION*,[6] I have described great many examples of men having succeeded in creating a reality to which they have aspired. One of the vital aspects of success, it was evident, was their ability to clearly visualize their desired result. Then, I suggest, they visualized having succeeded. Or, as the religious people would put it, they believed in having received the grace. Jesus put it more bluntly: "...all things, whatsoever you shall ask in prayer, believing, ye shall receive." The stress is, of course, on *believing*.

Visualization is the key.

If your faith in success is insufficient to create a clear picture of your desire, you cannot expect to have it manifest itself in objective reality. Another way of putting it is that you must create it—or bring it out of the virtual reality into your *subjective reality*—before it can be manifested in the *objective* reality, the reality we share with other people.

People expect to be given step-by-step instructions on how to procure results. This cannot be done. The general principles have been made available over the centuries, and the rest is up to us. No one can create subjective reality for us. Others can aid us in some small measure, but basically, this is tantamount to interference with our personal karma. Nevertheless, we can help others, but only when asked. To interfere with the subjective reality of someone else without authorization is equivalent to black magic—no matter how well intentioned.

Essentially, if we manage to create our subjective universe, the objective out-picturing of it will take care of itself. But we must not expect God nor any other divinity (saints nor saviors, angels nor demons, nor even Satan himself) to do it for us.

We must do it ourselves.

Only we have the key to the kingdom of our own subjective reality. We might choose to lend our key to someone, on occasion, but, sooner or later, we must learn to use the key ourselves. It is our kingdom. Yours and mine.

Such is our claim to abundant wealth. It is available to all. It is inexhaustible.

All you need is faith. In your Self.

***

010121

FOOTNOTES

(1). Acts of the Apostles 3:1-8.
(2). See also BEYOND RELIGION Volume I, *Creativity* (961219) and *Genesis* (970210). [Inhousepress, Montreal 1997, 2001, Amazon Kindle Edition 2010]
(3). John 14:14
(4). Compare "I in them, and thou in me, that they may be made perfect in one;" John 17:22
(5). In physicist's jargon, event-horizon denotes the point (line) of no return.
(6). VISUALIZATON—CREATING YOUR OWN UNIVERSE, [Inhousepress, Montreal 2001, Amazon Kindle 2010]

*One went to the door of the Beloved and knocked.
A voice asked, "Who is there?"
He answered, "It is I."
The voice said,
"There is no room for Me and Thee."
The door was shut.*

*After a year of solitude and deprivation
he returned and knocked.
A voice from within asked, "Who is there?"
The man said, "It is Thee."
The door was opened for him.*

Jalaluddin Rumi
[Idris Shah THE SUFIS [Doubleday, New York, 1964; pg. 317]

47

APRON STRINGS

This is the positively, absolutely and unequivocally the last time I raise the question of growing up.[1] In subject matters that are diametrically opposed to the established course of human thought, some repetition is irrevocable. This need for the examination of a new concept from many different angles is not a new penchant. No book is as repetitive as the greatest bestseller of all time: the Bible. Edgar Casey is said to have been reading the Bible continuously from cover to cover, one might say *ad nauseam*, or as many times as his relatively short life-span permitted. When asked which translation of the Bible is the best he replied, "The Bible is but one sentence, the rest are just illustrations how to incorporate this concept into our lives."[2]

I do not presume to compare my own thoughts to the Bible. In fact, it is the Bible that inspired and, I believe, supports my contentions. Where my contentions *may appear* to vary, perhaps, is in the stress I place on aspects which, 2000 years ago, the scribes of the Bible relegated to a later phase of our evolution. Briefly, during the first two millennia after Christ, we have been instructed to learn to love one another. This was imperative in preparation for the powers that are about to explode in our consciousness. We are not to give up our 2000 year-old lesson, but to take the next step.

We are to cut our apron strings.

We shall, whether we like it or not.

As has been concluded in my previous essays, so far, from the biological point of view, our evolution has been set on automatic. Darwin's theory of evolution, so despised by the religious fundamentalists, is still the guiding light in understanding our past. The pseudo-scientists (i.e.: ladies and gentlemen equivalent to closet-philosophers, or people who claim to know all the answers) think of Darwinism as a theory of pure chance. Nothing could be further from the truth. It is true that random mutations are a chance occurrence, but the vital part of the theory deals with deliberate and purposeful *selection*. Richard Dawkins, whose views on the subject are abbreviated above, calls the selection *sublimely and quintessentially non-random*.[3] Yet he attributes our (biological) survival to a computer program. This holds true for all our near cousins, elephants and monkeys, and for that matter, for oaks or pine trees. We all multiply after our own kind.[4] But whether we talk of the social or the antisocial (parasite) genes, they are all controlled by single software program with but one instruction: Duplicate Me. Not improve me, not advance me on the ladder of evolution, but regardless of my inherent qualities: *Duplicate Me*.[5]

And that's exactly what our genes do—and did, barring accidents (or unforeseen mutations), for some millions of years.

No more.
Not if we choose to have something to do with it.
This coming millennium will see changes so great as to upset the balance of nature. New software shall be written, with or without acquiescence of various powers at large. This is not a warning but a promise. The genie refuses to jump back into the test-tube (pun intended!). Our human gene will be manipulated, new attributes shall be added to it, other shall be removed. We shall cut our apron strings and venture on our own.

I repeat, it's a promise.

And that's not all.

Our new capabilities will open new vistas to fire our imagination still further. We shall dare to venture where "no man has gone before." We shall make many mistakes, take risks with the whole human species, indeed, play with fire. For a time, our power to alter our future will be much greater than our control over it. At least, at the early stages. The churches will scream that we are doing devil's work. The lesser minds already do. They will threaten us with God's wrath, with eternal damnation. So will a number of socio-political powerhouses, yet... when their own skins will be in danger, they will all beg for the 'miracles' of modern genetics.

Whatever else our genes are, they endow us with human nature.[6]

When the prophet of old said, "Ye are Gods," he had in mind the potential with which we have all been endowed. He was addressing the promise of consciousness yet to be awakened in our primitive minds and hearts. He had nothing to say as to how we shall flex our divinely inspired muscles, our divinely conceived minds. That latter part had to wait for the onset of the Age of Aquarius.

The Age is here now.

I hope the leading minds in the field of genetic manipulation will never forget that there is only one reason for evolution, and that is to furnish Consciousness with a better vehicle, a better instrument through which to experience the mode of becoming. To *experience* Life. They must never forget that God has no being but in a mode of being. We are now in position to influence this mode in heretofore unimaginable ways. The forces that govern the Age of Aquarius will assure that this new mode will be accessible and available to all.

We all have two choices. We can fulfill our destiny and become... "as gods", or we can be trampled by those who refuse to waste their divine heritage. It will not be easy. The greater our power, the greater danger attendant to lack of experience. We have but one safety factor. One single trait

which will protect us from each other, from the abuse with which such enormous power will tempt us. We had two thousand years to practice this divine trait, to metabolize it into our genetic code. By now, *we must have learned to love one another*.
I repeat, the genie will not jump back into the bottle. God help us if we haven't learned our lesson.

***

010125

FOOTNOTES

(1). To my unabashed shame, I'd since written a novel *Princess*, and then expanded it to the Alexander Trilogy consisting of *Alec*, *Alexander*, and *Sacha*. I only realized belatedly that growing up never end. That it goes on for ever...
(2). The one sentence was Christ's eleventh commandment, see John 15:12, 1 John 3:11, 2 John 5 et al. I cite Cayce from memory. The exact words may vary, the meaning is the same
(3). Dawkins, Richard CLIMBING MOUNT IMPROBABLE [W.W. Norton, New York 1996] p.80. It is this "sublimely and quintessentially non-random" selection which I compare in my other essays to the inherent predisposition towards order, harmony and beauty.
(4). Compare Genesis 1:11, 12, 34, 25, 6:20, 7:14.
(5). Dawkings, p.297-298.
(6). To be more accurate, we might accuse the DNA for our hereditary traits.

Post scriptum

Almost exactly one month after I wrote the above essay, on February 23, 2001, a *News Brief* in the *Montreal Gazette* reported that "eighty (80!) U.S. Nobel laureates have signed a letter to U.S. President George W. Bush urging him not to block the first flow of federal dollars for research on human embryo cells." (The human embryo cells concerns stem cells research). It is a telling case of brains versus stagnant establishment squirming to uphold the *status quo*.

48

PERCENTAGES

I read somewhere that **80%** of people in America are above average. No matter, the important thing is to make sure that you and I are right up there, with them. Right? Did you ever stop to think that 49% of university professors are probably below the average IQ of the university professors? And that the same goes for doctors of medicine, dentists, architects and illustrious members of all illustrious professions? 49% of all of them are below the average of all of them. In case of lawyers, their average is inversely proportional to the American average. Huhhh...?

The politicians are, of course, *all* below average. On average, that is.

But I have a word of cheer.

I do not believe that 49% of members of various organizations are below the average of the remaining 51% forming the majority. I rather think that approximately 999 members in every thousand, in anyone group, are below average. To equalize the equation, we must assign 99.9% of the brain-power to the leader and spread the remaining 0.01% among the sheep. It figures about right. Only we must never divulge this truth to the sheep. They do not mind how impoverished they are in certain upper quarters, providing no one tells them about it. Of course, if we do tell them, they might be in danger of rising above average. Like the Americans.

Decide for yourself.

Frankly, none of this matters much. Not much until you decide to run a gambling establishment, a hobby so popular among our politicians (the 0% group, remember?). When the gambling establishments calculate the odds of winning, they announce them openly, and rely on the IQ of their faithful voting fraternity to fill their coffers with silver. And the fraternity does. They wait in line to do so. They attend casinos, play lottos, shake hands with one-armed bandits, partake in any and every lottery in which the chances of winning are about the same as their intelligence quotient over a billion. Good enough to gamble, right? After all, *someone* has to win? Huhhh???

Someone usually does. But, not always. When no one wins, part of the loot is transferred to next week's winnings. Only next week twice as many people play, presumably reducing the odds. No matter, as long as they, themselves, are above average. Right?

Huhhh???

The political pollsters rely heavily on percentages. They claim to be accurate within 3%age points, 18 times out of 20. If your winning margin is 2%age points, then.... huh... they are *always* wrong? Well, always on average.

Yet our glorious leaders cannot make a decision without a poll. Even our overpaid newscasters on the idiot box ask: "tell us what you think?" I thought they were there to report on the news, not ask us to provide it. Anyway, whatever the answer the average (three or four) viewers will provide, the next day we shall be treated to their *average* decision. Within 3%age points, of course. 18 times out of a 100. Or less, on average.

Huh???

Percentages were OK when people were still able to count. Now we deal in generalities. In averages. The population of the world has grown. Permillages might be better. Or, perhaps, permillionages. After all, there are millions of people regularly wasting their time in front of their TVs, snugly guzzling beer while contemplating averages and popcorn. Something to do with baseball, I believe. Why would the newscasters be interested in the opinions of four or five guzzlers? Duhhh....

I guarantee that few people have any idea what I am talking about. On average, within, plus or minus, huh....? Why must we *be* percentages?

And this brings me to you and me.

Did you ever stop to think that if you don't belong to any group, you couldn't find yourself in the lower half of their average intelligence quotient? If you are just you, no title, no clique, horde, mob, throng, cluster, set, gang, camp, faction, syndicate, cartel, conglomerate, association, party, organization.... phew... then you are tops. The best—even without the crop. Not a bad place to be.

To achieve this distinction, you must, of course, be an individual. A title to which many lay claim but then spend the majority of their waking hours trying to fit into a group. A strange predilection yet practiced by virtually all. Yes, including my friends. Or at least my friends until they read this essay. My... ex-friends?

***

010127

*Two things are infinite:
the universe and human stupidity;
and I'm not sure about the universe*

Albert Einstein

49
TO KILL OR NOT TO KILL

Three-thousand-five-hundred years after Moses gave his people the Commandment *Thou shalt not kill*, and two-thousand years after Jesus of Nazareth advocated his followers to *never* judge one-another, but to *love one another* instead, the Vatican decided to issue a new, or at least a revamped, constitution which takes the death penalty off the Holy See's books. In fact Pope Paul VI already abolished the ultimate punishment within the walls of the Vatican City in 1960, but the official abolition will only be published in February 2001.

Until recently, officially, the Vatican stood shoulder-to-shoulder, saw eye-to-eye, with the likes of the freshly half-baked president of the world's most powerful country, George W. Bush, who firmly upholds the states prerogative to murder anyone it or they want to. While Pope John Paul II is strongly opposed to death penalty, the Vatican constitution, which dates back to the creation of the modern Vatican city-state in 1929, upheld the power to kill. Under Pope Pius IX (1792–1878), the Vatican continued to hang their undesirables well into the 19th century. Perhaps this is why Pius IX found it necessary to declare himself infallible.[1]

Apparently, things ain't as simple as they seem.

Krishna, speaking to Arjuna in the scriptural ballad Bhagavad-Gita, strongly advocates the prerogative of killing, providing it is done in the name of, and apparently for the benefit of Krishna, who represents the Hindû religion's

Supreme Deity.[2] In Chapter 18:59, Krishna says: "If you do not act according to My direction and do not fight, then you will be falsely directed. By your nature, you will have to be engaged in warfare." This tenor of absolute moral obedience is vaguely reminiscent of Abraham's willingness to kill his young son Isaac at his Lords command.[3] Setting aside any possible symbolic interpretation of both parables, I quote the renown authority on Hindû scriptures, Srila Prabhupada, who affirms the literal meaning of the Hindû scripture: "Arjuna was a military man, born with the nature of a *ksatriya*.[4] Therefore his natural duty was to fight." And thus, kill, no doubt. Srila Prabhupada states further that: "...because of *false ego* he (Arjuna) was thinking that there would be a sinful reaction from killing his teacher, grand-father and friends."[5] It is of some interest that the same scholar affirms that "Slaughter is the way of subhumans," but here, the swami is talking about "obtaining needed fat." In other words about killing the non-human animals.[6]

I hope more of us suffer from a sinful *false ego*.

It seems that the past popes of the Roman Church, when sanctioning the many crusades (11th to 14th c.) and a few centuries of gory inquisition have exercised exactly the same sentiment.[7] The logic adopted by the Roman church escapes me, since the commandment "thou shalt not kill" is quite clear.[8] The Hindûs, however, came up with a superb 'excuse'. They argue that since a murderer would, through the immutable laws of Karma, have to pay for his sin anyway, then why not kill him straight away and save the poor sap the necessity to forfeit his life later on. This would apply, however, only to killing the killers, but what of the non-killers? Like blasphemers, sexual abusers and/or perverts, and other practitioners of hobbies reserved by the heretics? In spite of the specificity of commandment, the Hebrews interpreted the Old Testament to afford total impunity for stoning to death such disagreeables.

So, the past popes were not alone. Blood-sports always had been "in" among the ruling classes. They still are.

The danger is that once we decide that we are killing by a specific directive of whatever deity we bow our knee to, we open a hornets' nest. We can always find a reason to get rid of whomever we find scurrilous, dangerous or just inconvenient to our cause. To our selected way of life. This is what all the extremists do. The Moslem, in the third-world countries, just like George W. Bush (until recently in the third-world Texas), continue to murder whoever breaks *their* law. They, the killers, always find a perfectly logical excuse (they call it reason) to hung 'em, stone 'em, get rid of 'em by a lethal injection or by other intricate method. The important thing is that we murder in the name of *something*. Sometimes it's the law, but usually... in the name of God. They never think of treating the purported transgressors for a 'deadly' disease.

Let me remind all the advocates of killing, of another promise made us by one who endeavored to dissuade us from our bloodthirsty habits. He said that all that fight with the sword will die by the sword. Or by hanging. Or lethal injection. Or on an electric chair with all the modern trimmings and up-to-date technology.

If not in this life, then the next.

But they will die.

What say you, Mr. President?

***

010128

FOOTNOTES

(1). The doctrine of papal infallibility has been enunciated at the First Vatican Council (1869—1870).

(2). Bhagavad-Gita, AS IT IS, Translations and purports by His Divine Grace A.C. Bhaktivedanta Swami Prabhupada [The Bhaktivedanta Book Trust, Los Angeles, 1976]

(3). Genesis 22:2.

(4). BHAGAVAD-GITA, *Ksatriya*—the administrative and protective occupation according to the system of four social and spiritual orders. [ibid. p.281]. We must remember that India still "enjoys" a cast system.

(5). ibid, p.269.

(6). ibid. p.248.

(7). The medieval Inquisition began c.1233 and became really bloody under Ferdinand and Isabella of Spain (established in 1478) In 1542 pope Paul III assigned the medieval Inquisition to the modern Congregation of the Holy Office, where it resides to this day.

(6). Exodus 20:13

Heaven and earth shall pass away,
but my words shall not pass away.

Matthew 24:35

50

MANIPULATORS

Still during the pre-Solidarity days, my wife left Poland because she felt manipulated. She chose the unknown, the uncertain, a future fraught with danger. The others stayed behind and for them, not much had changed during the last few-thousand years—perhaps longer. For as long as people walked the earth there have been manipulators and those, the vast majority, who have been content to be manipulated. The manipulees. The manipulators had knowledge that they continued to guard jealously, others preferred the line of least resistance—the life of abject ignorance.

As I said, not much has changed.

Manipulators and manipulees continue to coexist in the same old love/hate relationship. The users and the used seem unable to break the vicious circle of their inherent limitations. The manipulators know that should the masses learn what they know, they would refuse to be manipulated. Since my wife left Poland, communism had fallen. New (often the same but under a different guise) manipulators took over their predecessors' function.

Two thousand years ago, Jesus rebelled against such manipulation. Not against the Romans whose iniquitous ways limited the physical freedom of his brethren, but against those manipulators who subjugated his people's minds. Jesus was not a religious man. He respected the Spiritual Law, not the laws created by the manipulators of the biblical writings. Sabbath was created for man, he'd said, not man for Sabbath.

He believed that the laws of Torah were supposed to enhance life, not subjugate men to serve the few holding the key of knowledge contained therein. He even accused the Pharisees (and lawyers) of being fools who have the knowledge of good life, a life of freedom, yet they neither used it themselves nor did they share it with others.[1]

Not much has changed...

For almost two thousand years the Roman church took over the function of the Pharisees, of keeping their minions in abject ignorance. A number of my preceding essays offer ample evidence to back this thesis. Until recently, the faithful have been even forbidden to read the Old Testament, without a special dispensation. After all, had they read it, they might have started thinking for themselves. And that the manipulators could not permit. Their ability to control others would have been seriously compromised. To be fair, the 'manipulees' also avoided mental effort at all cost.

According to the manipulators, Bhagavad-Gita affirms that people are born into castes with predetermined limitations (hereditary social classes), and therefore must function within, and assume the obligations assigned to, each caste. So, the manipulators claim, commands Krishna, the Supreme Personality of Godhead. They carefully forget Krishna's words that *"The Supreme Lord is situated in everyone's heart,"* thus denying any and all limitations, castes, or religious impositions.[2] *"Give up all varieties of religion and just surrender unto Me. ...you have nothing to fear,"* says Krishna.[3] Not much about castes, rules and regulations. *"Follow me"* says the Christ, *"Let not your heart be troubled, neither let it be afraid."*[4] Nothing here about any rules, regulations or religion either.

People didn't follow the Christ, nor surrender to Krishna, for that matter. Instead, over the centuries, they chose to remain obediently supine, prone, if you prefer. Not before Christ or Krishna.

Before (or behind) the manipulators.

People have always been content to serve whoever upheld and protected the *status quo*. They prefer to pay their tithes and leave thinking to others. No wonder the Hindûs maintained their caste system. It seemed a natural course. For their part, the Roman church exploited the warning "not to cast pearl before swine" to the full. They forgot that they themselves walked in the footsteps of their pharisaic predecessors. Jesus died to set *us* free. Religions replaced the old handcuffs with the new. They called them the Church Commandments, the Office of the Holy Inquisition, and volumes of theological mumbo-jumbo, of mysteries. All, for our good. For our good... in the next life.

What about this life?

Not much has changed.

But truly, is it still possible to keep knowledge from people? Are we still as ignorant, as mentally stagnant and lazy, as the various present-day manipulators would have us believe?

In 1534, the English monarch Henry VIII decided that, for his people, one puppet is as good as another. Of late, Britain faced quite a different problem. Various manipulators stood shoulder to shoulder to ban any and all genetic research. Their manipulations resulted in prolonged mass-hysteria directed against the horror of any tinkering with the genetic form of wheat or corn, let alone the human genome. Yet, recently, the House of Lords passed a law that legalizes "the devils work." The scientists will 'create' human embryos to extract their nascent stem cells. How could such legislation have been made possible?

By letting people in on the truth!

The drug and bio-chemical companies "stepped aside to allow patients' groups to spearhead the political battle." The effort of finding a cure for Parkinson's disease, cystic fibrosis or cancer was best lead by the sufferers from Parkinson's disease, cystic fibrosis or cancer. Their arguments carried weight. The scaremongers, the manipulators, always bent on the maintenance of *status quo*, were afraid to argue publicly against the patients. The manipulators were afraid of being accused of sentencing the sufferers to suffering and certain death. It was that simple.

It seems that knowledge can be entrusted to people. What of the rest of the world?

Dr. Margaret Somerville of Montreal's McGill Centre for Medicine, Ethics and Law warns that in doing such work "we could destroy the human spirit."[5] Is she really afraid of the immortal spirit suddenly becoming mortal through genetic research? Or is she just manipulating public opinion to avoid saying: don't roil the water, I'm alright, thank you.

We are growing up. As we reject the fetters imposed on us by the political, religious, economic and pseudo-scientific manipulators, we shall partake in the creative process for which the evolution has equipped us. The natural selection of that which is good and holy will come to the fore.

And we shall partake in the dawn of a new area.

***

010130

FOOTNOTES

(1). Matthew 23:13, Luke 11:52. See also Luke 12:1-3.

(2). Bhagavad-Gita - AS IT IS, 18:61. [The Bhaktivedanta Book Trust, Los Angeles 1968].

(3). Ibid. 18:66.

(4). Matthew 8:22 and John 14:27.

(5). This quotation and other genetic research data have been gleamed from an article by Bruce Wallace, Eurofile, [The Gazette, Montreal January 29, 2001]

51

TRINITY

[Only for readers who enjoy myths]

It probably all started with the sacred syllable AUM, the Medic Trimurti. The secret sound conceals the unrevealed Deity, the Swayambhouva, That which is That, That which has Its Being in and of Itself. Emanating from this ineffable Deity, the initial Source, the germ of the universe, are the three-in-one trinities forming a Supreme Whole. From AUM thus emanate the Nara, Nari and Viradyi, the initial triad. The Agni, Vaya and Sourya, the manifested triad that follows is still secret, intangible, esoteric.
The next Trimurti gave birth to religions.[1]

Hindûism, occasionally referred to as Brahmanism, offers us the first prequel of what was to come, of other religions that would follow, centuries later, including the dominant version of the Western Christianity.[2] Modern Hindûism offers us their Trinity as represented by the Brahma, the Vishnu and Siva (or Shiva), the *creative* triad. The Veda (the Brahmanas and the Bhagavad-Gita) proffers an elaborate commentary on the Trinity. Although around 550 BC, Brahmanism substituted a complex system of theology and ritual for the original Vedic literature, the original scriptures offer an exciting background, perhaps the origin, on which the Christians based some of their insights many centuries later.

Brahma, a distant, inaccessible deity, is often equated with the universe He has created. Brahma in no way differs from God the Father of the Old Testament. In the first book of the Old Testament, the Genesis, He 'single-handedly' created the universe.[3] As, "the Vedas have now been proved by scholars to antedate the Jewish Bible by many ages," one can but wonder where the Hebrews got their idea.[4] Where the New Testament differs from the Old and the Hindû version is that in the later rendering, Brahma/Father needs a means, an instrument, through which the act of creation takes place.

Vishnu is the Preserver.

This deity maintains that which has already been created in a state of relative existence. In previous essays, this process is maintained by the force of Life Itself. If the process were to be personified, then indeed Vishnu fits the bill admirably. We must remember that all old religions invariably relied on personification to make their gods more accessible to the masses. Perhaps they were right. No matter what Jesus had said about himself, the Christians still insist that He was god. A tough act to follow if you accept Jesus' comments regarding those who will come after him.[5]

Finally we come to Siva (Shiva).

Though Siva is referred to as the destroyer, I would suggest that, as in Buddhism, the only destruction that takes place is of one's ego. Indeed, the final or complete return to the heavenly state of consciousness is impossible while we retain any vestiges of ego. After all, heaven is a 'virtual' state of consciousness, and there is nothing virtual about ego. So if Siva and his bride Kali destroy this world, it is only to make room for the new, even as we relinquish our bodily cells, atoms and subatomic particles on a continual basis, to make room for new cells to take their place. We now know that the human body replaces its cellular structure in cycles of around 54 weeks, while the constituent parts, the subatomic particles, wink in and out of existence in minute fractions of a second. All thanks to Siva.

This is, perhaps, why some Hindû scholars often refer to the Veda as science.

A deeper analysis will allow us to assign to Siva one other attribute, that which we now refer to as Love. It is thanks to Siva that the circle can be closed, that that which has been manifested, created, can revert to the original source, perhaps to serve as building blocks for new manifestations.

On our journey toward the Judeo-Christian concepts, we enter the valley of Tigris and Euphrates that became known as Mesopotamia. Here we find ourselves on more familiar ground, first recorded in Genesis 24:10, when Abraham sent his servant (together with ten camels) in search of a wife. The Chaldeans of Mesopotamia (in Hebrew meaning of or between two rivers) had their own version of the Trinity, most likely also preceding that of the Hebrews.[6] We find the Chaldean Trinities strangely reminiscent of the Vedic version. Even as in India, Brahma who incorporates the male and female principles (Nara and Nari) gave birth to the Son, Vardji, the creative principle, so the Ilu from whom emanated the androgynous Eikon (incorporating the male Anu and the female Anata) eventually producing the trinity of Any, Bel and Hoa, directly correspond to Brahma, Vishnu and Siva. Both the Hindu and the Chaldean trinities blended into One: Brahmä and Anu respectively, through the intercession of the Hindû Virgin Nari and the Chaldean Virgin Mylitta. Thus we have the precedent for the Christian version of the Virgin Mary giving birth to the Christ.

It's a small world.

Without engaging in an argument on chronology, we must mention the Egyptian triunes, which likewise date back to well before the Hebrew area. The Egyptian Trinities also ensue from the non-manifested Osiris, Isis and Horus, to the manifested Ra, Isis, and Malouli,[7] corresponding to the very familiar if, comparatively speaking simplistic Christian version of Father, Mother and Son. But if we reverse the order and substitute Spirit for Mother, we have the orthodox

Christian trinity of Father, Son and the Holy Ghost. The matter becomes somewhat confused, since, as the Christian God is one, Mother Mary must have given birth to both the Son and the Father, a matter of some chronological and/or sequential difficulty. This problem became such a nuisance that during the 9th century the Christian church decided to revise their original Credo of the First Council of Nicæa in 325 in an attempt to resolve the issue.[8] There they stated that "The Holy Ghost proceedeth from the Father and the Son" rather than the other way round. No matter. The popes only became infallible much later.[9]

Perhaps this is the right time and place to stress, that this does not aspire to be a scholarly and/or authoritative expose of the mythological Triuns throughout history of man, but rather a sketch to whet readers' appetite for the subject discussed. The complexities of any one mythology give ample opportunity for a full tome of research and analysis, without any guarantee of a successful synthesis. Such is the nature of the subject matter. We search for the unknown. Some say, the Unknowable. I dare to dispute the latter. We are part of the Unknown. Thus It is an integral part of our ground of Being.

Back to the murky past.

The Hebrew seemed satisfied to subsist on a single ineffable Divinity expressed by the tetragrammaton YHWH, which incorporates the male and female principles, rather like the Brahma of the Hindûs or the Eikon of the Chaldeans. However, if we delve into their esoteric mysteries of the Kabala[10], we find that the God of Israel is only the third emanation of the ineffable Divinity. While the earliest texts of Kabala are reputed to coincide with those of the earliest Christian writings, the Kabala concerns itself with the esoteric interpretation of still earlier knowledge, which appears to have been lost in remote antiquity.

The Hindû Brahma is known to the Cabalists as En-Soph (the unrevealed or the non-existent one) from whom proceeded successive emanations. According to H.B. Blavatsky, the cabalistic trinity if one of the models of the Christian one.[11] In spite of my repeated readings, their full inner meaning eludes me. I shall therefore quote Franck, the translator of the Kabala:

"The ten Sephiroth are divided into three classes, each of them presenting to us the divinity under a different aspect, the whole still remaining an *indivisible Trinity*. The first three Sephiroth are purely intellectual.... The three that follow... are named the virtues, or the sensible world. Finally... the last three Sephioroth... constitute the natural world, or nature in its essence and the active principle."[12]

I am sure that a deeper study would reveal a greater intimacy with the Christian Trinity, but, apparently, only to better minds than mine. Perhaps it might suffice to say that the En-Soph of Kabala corresponds exactly to the Hindû AUM, and that ultimately we end up with successive Trinities that progressively manifest their presence in our mundane universe.

Complex, esoteric, presumably meant to edify us.

Please feel edified!

***

010131

FOOTNOTES

(1). Trimurti, Sanskrit from *tri* meaning three, and *mûrrti* meaning body or shape.

(2). Not to confused with the original teaching of Christ.

(3). At least 'single-handedly' in the 'improved' English version of the Bible. In Hebrew, God—the Mighty One is *El*. God—the Object of Worship is *ELAH*. God—Objects of Worship (plural) is *ELOHIM*, which is or are the gods that created the universe in the first verse and chapter of Genesis.

(4). Blavatsky, H.P. ISIS UNVEILED, Vol. I—*Science*. [1988 Theosophical University Press, Pasadena, California]; p.91].

(5). John 14:12

(6). refer to Kapuscinski, Stanislaw DICTIONARY OF BIBLICAL SYMBOLISM [Inhousepress 2001, also available as eBook]

(7). Although some scholars (Champollion) assert that the starting point of the Egyptian mythology is the triad of Kneph, Neith, and Phtah.

(8). In 1997 I have discussed the subject in somewhat greater detail in my essay on *Myth and Reality* BEYOND RELIGION I [Inhousepress Montreal 1997, 2001)

(9). As late as 19th century under Pius IX.

(10). or Cabbala meaning in Hebrew: Reception.

(11). Blavatsky, H.P. ISIS UNVEILED, Vol. II—Theology. [1988 Theosophical University Press, Pasadena, California; pg. 222].

(12). ibid. page 40. (my emphasis)

One who speaks about the Trinity lies!

Meister Eckhart

52

BEYOND RELIGION III

A PERSONAL VIEW

Everything already exists in its *potential* **form.**
 Whatever we, for a minute fragment of eternity, endow with reality, is of little consequence to the Whole. It will, however, shape *our* individual perception. Only in this sense our belief system matters—because it adds texture to the fabric of our life. If the reality we devise enriches our perception, our 'accessibility' to the Whole, that aspect, that fragmentary boon becomes immortal, eternal, with our name inscribed on our contribution.[1] If our 'contribution' is limited to the sustaining of that which already is, if it does not break new ground, is not instrumental in bringing aspects of virtual reality into the manifested reality, it is as though we haven't lived. We do not suffer for eternity, as some charlatans would have us believe yet we, as we were in that particular reincarnation, just simply don't exist.

That is why shaping our reality on the premises of Universal Truths is so vital in the most precise meaning of the word. Vital. Necessary for our survival. And let us make no mistake about it. Every human is endowed with a very specific, inimitable ability to contribute to the Whole. It may be a singular work of art which strikes a chord of subliminal understanding in others, it may be singular act of joy— brought to one in need and propagated at an elusive moment of eternity; it may be being instrumental in aiding someone in performing their unique gift of unfoldment. It is never limited to sustaining the human species on this overpopulated planet. It is always directly related to the unfoldment of Spirit, not to the unfoldment of flesh. The material world is set on automatic, it requires little or no assistance from us to continue on its meandering course.[2] The Selfish Gene will take care of the flesh.[3] Stars will be born and they'll die, without our assistance. But the virtual universe, the heaven, the Ocean of Infinite Possibilities needs us for Its unfoldment, even as we need It for our individual survival, or perhaps better said, of the survival of our individuality.

It is in this spirit that I offer my own version of Trinity.

Not in contrast or opposition to the many Triunes of the past, but rather in an attempt to 'update' them all through our new understanding which has been growing in our mind during the ongoing procession of the Zodiac. The Trinity I offer consists of Light, Life and Love. And the Three, as all the Trinities of the hoary past, are One. They are no longer personified in entities outside our own being, but rather having their being in us and through us. As stated many times throughout this collection of essays, God has no being other than in a mode of being. You and I are such mode. We are the chosen ones. The ones consciously aware of our mission, our purpose.

In Hebrew philosophy, the initial symbolic awakening took place on the day on which Isaac became Israel.

It is a charming story which, from the evolutionary standpoint, corresponds to the light which pierced the august shadows of the Bo tree to flood Buddha's consciousness.[4] The moment of enlightenment does not come with a thunderous, cataclysmic earthquake. The Armageddon is long past. The enlightenment, first of many, comes in a single ray of Light, an arrangement of photons which convey the Single Truth to us, often in small, palatable portions.

The Awakening is an ongoing process.
A process of Eternal Unfoldment.

People who are motivated by materialistic philosophy find their whole brain at their disposal. After all, it took billions of years to evolve a brain that could co-ordinate and assure physical survival. As I had written in my book *VISUALIZATION*, our bodies with all their appurtenances are created "unto the image of God,"[5] The *manifested* God, of course. Physical survival is our brain's primary, if not sole, purpose.[6] The brain is little more than a fantastic calculating machine: fully automated with ample memory storage. To reach beyond the material, we must, by definition, reach beyond the intellectual, beyond the logical, beyond whatever our brain disposes and enables us to achieve. The science of tomorrow is the magic of today. Again I must stress: the *only* purpose of our brain is to assure our *physical* survival. It cannot add a cubit to our height.[7] It cannot extend our life beyond certain predetermined limits. Often it can't even aid us in curtailing a destructive habit, in spite of our knowledge and apparent willingness. Exactly the same function is ascribed by nature to the brain, no matter how large or small, of every animal. To experience the transcendental we must, in a way, diminish the efficacy of our brain, or, at the very least, to bypass its primary function. We are nudged towards that end by the concept of Trinity, this time at the individual level, and this concept will lead us to Jacob and the mystical Trinity of Is-ra-el.[8]

Why Trinity?

This enigmatic trio seems to permeate the days of yore. Yet it is as fresh today as it must have been before the beginning of time. It is the necessary triumvirate of stages of consciousness without which neither the universe nor you nor I could ever experience the mode of becoming. We shall soon see that once we forsake the Cosmological Trinities of the past, we shall enter the eternal Trinity of an individualized Soul.

There are three phases in the evolution of human consciousness. The first has been dragged out over billions of years. It has been so very slow, because the purpose of our brain is not to advance our race, but to sustain it. "If it ain't broke, don't fix it" seems to be the evolutionary motto. Thus only when our (physical) survival has been threatened, we made advances in our biological evolution. Nevertheless, this phase has advanced us beyond the necessity of allotting all our time to an eat-or-be-eaten mode of existence.

It brought us to the luxury of free time.[9]

The second phase, equally as vital though so short as to be not merely transient but practically ephemeral, finds its expression in the realm of religion. This is when we become aware of our potential. We look beyond our immediate needs, our mundane wants, likes and dislikes, and stretch a tentative hand outside our pre-established mode of being. We become aware that the act of becoming is not merely physical but it carries other, less tangible overtones, which we might, one-day, explore. We are taught how to control our thoughts, our emotions, how to recognize that the universe we inhabit overlaps with many other universes, ultimately forming a single, integral, indivisible Whole. But this is the concluding chapter of the second phase. For many—yet to be reached.

The third and last phase, stretching into infinity, requiring the adoption of the concept of immortality, lies *BEYOND RELIGION*. Any religion.

It lies beyond duality.

The first two phases are well known to all interested in such matters. Anthropology, paleontology and ancient history in general, continue to define the first. The second, though in cosmological terms conspicuously transient, also encompass great many ages, though substantially fewer than the first stage. We might think of the second stage as a transition from the first to the last, though in a deeper sense, this transition is an on-going process of continuous unfoldment. Yet the abundance of various religions, past and present, attest to the intensity and vitality of this fiery drama. Practically all religions lay claim to exclusive righteousness, to exclusivity over Truth, or, at the very least, to offering the shortest way to arrive at the Final Solution, usually referred to as heaven or paradise. The only aspect on which all religions find themselves in total agreement is their pitiful inability to define what that Final Solution, this enigmatic heaven is.

Yet this evanescent phase is of most vital importance.

It is here, in the realm of transient religions that people climb the ladder of eternal becoming, until, rightly or wrongly, they are compelled to become messengers of God. Or so they think. At the first whiff of the sweet fragrance of Truth we inhale the singularity of being with such savor, that we get drunk on the elixir of Life. We seem transported to intangible realms lost in the music of the spheres.[10] Yet, for as long as we remain *messengers* of God, we espouse duality. To deliver a message we must depart from Him whose message we are, purportedly, carrying. We must depart from the Source, thus assume separation as a state of being. We are still in the dichotomous, bewildering, field of battle. We still suffer, fight, struggle, arrogantly espouse opposition to evil, insist on the exclusivity of our way in the name of a single Source which, to our chagrin, continues to deliver such divergent messages through countless other messengers.

Alas, the Source *is* One. The messengers are many.

And the messages...? The messages are narrowed and distorted by the limitation of the human mind and language, by our ability to understand. Finally... we give up. And in this singular moment we are faced with the Triune, the Trinity, long suspected by countless religions. Only the Triune does not bear a human face. In fact It bares no face at all. These Three are neither limited nor contained in any man, woman nor child. We can but aspire to them. They are Light, Life and Love. The three in One. As Deepak Chopra once said, You are That, I am That—and That's all there is.

Thou shalt have no other gods before me. Nor before you.

The ancients have known this concept of the Three-in-One Trinity from time immemorial. To the Western man it came under the guise of Christianity, which preaches the

Triune of the Father, the Son and the Holy Ghost. A closer scrutiny of the New Testament reveals the Three-in-One concept rather well defined. The Father, the Source of All, the non-judgmental (For the Father judges no man)[11], non-opinionated (God is no respecter of persons)[12], incredibly prolific (...all things, whatsoever ye shall ask in prayer, believing, ye shall receive)[13], sounds very much like our Ocean of Infinite Possibilities, wherein all exists in a virtual state but needs a means, *an effort on our part* to manifest Itself in the universe we call our own.

The second person of the Trinity of the Christian version is epitomized by the Christ. I am life, he said of himself. Life can be defined as the means of imbuing the state of becoming on the "kingdom which is not of this world."[14] According to the Christian teaching, we can be instrumental in this Kingdom manifesting itself here and now. "Thy Kingdom come..." we are told to pray. We are *not* instructed to *go* to the Kingdom but to work for *the Kingdom to come to us*. A subtle twist on the accepted promulgation yet such twists destroy the very essence of Christ's teaching. The various churches managed to impose a complex ritual and theology on the original teaching, rather as the Brahmans did on the original Veda. No matter. Even after countless transcriptions the Truth still shines through. And the essence of the original teaching is that the second 'person' of the Trinity is Life Itself.[15]

Finally the third 'person', the Holy Spirit.

It is vital to come to a precise understanding of the third 'person'. It is not easy to discuss the Ghost, or Spirit. After all, It is intangible, ineffable. It can be neither seen, smelled, heard nor touched. It is as though It didn't exist in our world. We hear of good and bad spirits, of willing spirit, of being filled with spirit. Apparently we can act in good or bad spirit too. We can be out of spirits, poor in spirit; we can be filled with public spirit. We also have an abundance of chemical spirits—of salt, orange, camphor and many other. Supposedly we can also become a bit of a prankster spirit and haunt unsuspecting ignoramuses in old, dilapidated castles, particularly around the 31st of October. Spirits galore. Which of the spirit was Jesus alluding to when he bade us to watch out?

None of the above.

According to the gospel of Matthew, Jesus made a strange statement. He claimed that we can sin and blaspheme all we want and it shall be forgiven us, but if we blasphemed against the Holy Spirit—we cooked our goose.[16] Offend God the Father, God the Son and get away with it? Apparently. But not the Holy Ghost. Neither in this world nor the next. The admonition is easier to understand if we equate the Spirit with Love. Suffice to say that no attribute carries as much force, is as often repeated in the Christian scriptures, as that of Love. Faith, Hope and Charity, but the greatest of these is Love. Charity, Agape, the impersonal Love. It has been stressed in the scriptures on many occasions that without Love man cannot enter the Kingdom of Heaven.

By trifling with this concept, indeed with the significance of Love, we play a dangerous, in fact, deadly game. Love is our ticket to heaven, and only heaven assures us of immortality. All else is transient.

More about love later.

***

In my previous essay we discussed Cosmological Trinities, concepts so high above our puny comprehension that no good Hindû, Buddhist or Christian would attempt to equate himself with any aspect of such illustrious Triunes. Buddha is as much God to the Buddhists as Christ is to Christians. To the Hindûs, Brahma is as unattainable as any member of the Christian Trinity is to an average Christian. A Jew might dream of being another Moses and lead his people to an improbable peace in the Middle East, but none would aspire to equate themselves with the essence of YHWH. And yet, their own scripture give them ample encouragement to rise above mediocrity.

All they must do is to recall the story of Jacob.

And now, with some trepidation, I wish to offer the reader the de-personified trinity. With trepidation, because all knowledge carries power and power can be abused. Nevertheless only you can imbue this trinity with reality. The trinity of Light, Life and Love.

LIGHT

Light is an ancient symbol for Knowledge, and Knowledge is only available to consciousness. Light or Knowledge is not an accumulation of facts, data, but the omnipresent potential of everything, past-present-future, already existing in a potential or virtual state. The nuclear physicists assure us that what they deemed, heretofore, as vacuum, or empty space, is saturated with *virtual* subatomic particles, popping in and out of existence in unimaginably small fractions of a second. Other theoretical cosmologists postulate, or at the very least propose, virtual worlds, countless, infinite, all seemingly ready to become manifest in the tangible reality. This space, this 'vacuum' is the resplendent Ocean of Infinite Possibilities, a spring that can never run dry. For all we know, It is eternally replenished by the Black Holes that might well be returning their captured matter/energy to the Source, to the 'Vacuum', to the Ocean.

It is an Ocean of Virtual Existence. Whatever we want we can conjure from this Source. Eternal, Timeless, Invisible, Silent, Impersonal, Omnipresent, Omniscient, Non-judgmental, Limitless. Like LIGHT Itself. Like disembodied Consciousness.

Reminds you of anything?

And then there is Individualization: the divine attribute we know as Soul. The limitless possibilities of the limitless ocean remain just possibilities until they become individualized in Consciousness. More so, until this

Consciousness becomes embodied, exemplified, one could almost say—materialized. Until the virtual becomes real, until that which is possible becomes manifest. Until the Eternal I AM descends from the state of BEING into the transient state of BECOMING.

You and I embody this state. Consciously or not, we are the embodiment of virtual reality. A sudden awareness of that which we always suspected but never had the courage to admit. Even to ourselves. You and I *are* the Truth.

You and I are the embodiments of I AM.

When we accept that we are beings of Light—inhabitants of 'vacuum'—we are instantly released from any limitations imposed by the Theory of Relativity. We are beyond constrains of time and space, even of the velocity of light. We are 'virtual' beings, free, capable of manifesting our presence, or to assuage our consciousness in the material world in the past or future, in any form of shape, here and now, or on the furthest planet of the furthest galaxy. We are free. From among the many electromagnetic particles populating the theory of Quantum Mechanics, photon has no mass.

LIFE

We release the energy of electrons by withdrawing our control over them. By keeping 'still', our thoughts release their hold over the structural complexity, giving rise for collisions between the constituent particles of our bodies. Thus photons are emitted. In the ultimate degree of this process we become made up of photons, of light. Our higher consciousness, it appears, has the ability to retain and maintain control over these photons. Thus by 'relaxing' we 'quicken' the substance which we temporarily inhabit.

Ego, the concept of Self, is necessary for the experience of change.

Heaven is a static condition. It is a condition of eternal readiness, without imposing its will, its potential, until called for. It is like an eternal giver without ever asking anything in return. It is as the rain falling on the good and the bad, as the sun supplying its salutary rays for all that reach out for them. Thus, in the very same sense, both heaven and the Spirit are static. They both confer on consciousness the state of being. One is the source, the latter the means. Only ego can change that into the state of becoming. The price is the loss, albeit temporary, of the sense of Oneness. Yet only the ego, the *individualized consciousness*, the individualized Soul, can produce change, can aspire to new ways, new systems, and new forms. Only in Ego State can the consciousness partake in the creative process of converting the virtual in the tangible. And, as we shall soon see, only Love spans the modes of being and becoming. It defines the state of being and motivates the exigencies of becoming.

In the tangible, material universe we see through our mortal eyes all things, plants, animals and people alike, in a state of constant decay.[17] In the truest sense, we, and the universe around us, are dead. *Life is a condition of eternal becoming.* Continuous exfoliation, the coming forth, the act of the virtual becoming tangible—only to die, to fall to decadence in the very moment of creation. It is as Iago cried: From the moment of birth I am in a state of corruption.[18] Physically, we all are. What lives on is the Process, impersonally supervised by our Higher Consciousness.

What lives is Life Itself.

LOVE

As mentioned before, contrary to many who consider that scientists took upon themselves to oppose religions, or metaphysical thought, I see the scientific community to have contributed more of our understanding of the unknown, to many the unknowable, than their counterparts in the religious community. In the 'pre-scientific' society, priesthood had pursued the conquest of knowledge. Even then, as now, they agreed that the greatest *unifying force in the universe* is Love. It is *sine qua non* for the continuity of existence. Of immortality. We can think of Love, therefore, as the Unifying Force that spans the bridge between the individualized unit of consciousness and the Field of Origin, whence it came.

We tend to separate our own mental states, our wealth, attributes, forever stressing that which keeps us apart. To delve into the real meaning of Love, we must attempt to understand that there is only One Consciousness, even as there is only One Soul. This Single Consciousness, the attribute of the 'Unified Field', of Heaven, manifests the ability to individualize Itself into seemingly countless components. This ability we refer to as Soul. At the ground of being, 'your' soul and 'my' soul are one. We are both infinitely minute components of the Whole. And there is yet another treat in stall for us. The studies of many mystics of the past (some of the present), reveal that while we are indivisible components of a great Whole, *qualitatively* the Whole is present in Its *TOTALITY* in every aspect or component of Its being.

As God is All in All, than such Allness permeates every aspect of God.

The Dharma-Body in the hedge at the bottom of the garden of the Zen Masters is nothing less than finding All in All. To meet God face to face is to find God in a frog, in a single bloom of a flower, in the eyes of one's beloved. God is not a person, never was, but is present in Its totality in every person. In you and me, in our friends and enemies alike. Since everything emanates from a single Source, be it Father, or Brahma, or God, there is nothing outside God.

This ability to perceive this Suchness is offered by the force of Love.

Thus, while observing love in its many diluted manifestations, in inter-human relations, in the attractions to higher aspirations, art, creativity—fundamentally Love has but one purpose: to take us back whence we came. To close the loop, to re-establish conscious relationship of unity of all.

Not just among people of earth, among the things dear and familiar to us, but with the whole of the manifested universe.

The spirit that guaranties us the re-entry into a mode of immortality is also That which opens the gate into the original state of consciousness from which we all emerged. The original virtual state, is the state of being that, through the attribute of Life, enabled us to individualize ourselves into a mode of becoming. The Spirit enables us to revert to our roots, to Eden, to the eternal state of being. The Spirit Jesus was taking about is synonymous with Love. We might call It, the Spirit of Love.

Only Love can open the doors to the Ocean of Infinite Possibilities.

Only Love guaranties us immortality.

A parting thought.

If anyone attempts to separate the three attributes of Light, Life and Love and personalize them, they will regress by not less than 5000 years.

***

010210

FOOTNOTES

(1). Revelation 3:12
(2). It helps if we do not continually abuse our bodies with mental, emotional and particularly physical gluttony.
(3). A term coined by Richard Dawakins in his bestseller THE SELFISH GENE (1976, 1989)
(4). The Bo tree was aptly named, much later, *Ficus religiosa*.
(5). Kapuscinski, Stanislaw VISUALIZATION—*Creating Your Own Universe*, [Inhousepress, Montreal 2001].
(6). Beyond the obvious, the brain remains open to random mutations and partakes in the process of selection and the resulting genetic survival.
(7). Matth.6:27.
(8). See Kapuscinski, Stanislaw BEYOND RELIGION Vol.I, *Self* (970102) [Inhousepress, Montreal 1997, 2001]

(9). By inference, the people we refer to as workaholics are not fulfilling their destiny. They could be called psychological mutants, veering on a wrong tangent.

(10). Compare Gospel of Thomas, [NAG HAMMADI LIBRARY] Logion 13. See also Kapuscinski, Stanislaw THE KEY TO IMMORTALITY, [Inhousepress, Montreal 2001, Amazon Kindle Edition 2010]

(11). John 5:22

(12). Acts 10:34

(13). Matthew 21:22; compare Matthew 7:7, Mark 11:24, Luke 11:9, et al.

(14). John 18:36

(15). "I am the resurrection, and the life: he that believeth in me, though he were dead, yet shall he live: and whosoever liveth and believeth in me shall never die." John 25-26 et al.

(16). Matthew 12:31—32.

(17). Those whose eyes have been *opened*, see the unfolding process itself. The experience is as euphoric as the experience of the other attributes of the Triune.

(18). Iago's monologue (*Credo in un Dio crudel che m'ha creato...*) Giuseppe Verdi's Otello, Act 2.

*I don't really want to write about
"spiritual things."*

*The words sound too empty and trivial.
I just don't feel like spinning out a lot of words about God
and prayer. I feel in fact immensely poor and fallible, but I
don't worry about it.
I just live.*

Thomas Merton
SCHOOL OF CHARITY, 1966
[3rd volume of Merton's letters, selected & edited by Patrick Hart; pg. 323]

POSTSCRIPT

While I had offered my vision of heaven, it must be stressed that the perception of heaven can and should be interpreted at different levels of experience. Even within my own 'version' the degrees of understanding can range from a purely scientific pursuit of the subject all the way to a mystic experience, which cannot be put into words.

The first, most immediate heaven can be recognized in the 'void'. This view, often erroneously attributed to Buddha, offered no 'vision' until the scientists discovered that the void is not empty. In fact, they say, it is replete with virtual particles that wink in and out of existence in, reputedly, 10^{-21} of a second.[1] A truly minuscule fragment of eternity. It is as if they didn't exist at all. But they do. They constantly offer themselves to be caught and sustained in a manifested reality by any consciousness capable of so doing. It appears, however, that the influence of such a consciousness is not limited to a willful intervention, and is in fact energized by, what the religions call, faith, which I prefer to define as an ability to visualize the new manifestation with total commitment to its reality.

Nevertheless, without the intervention of consciousness the world as we know it (and an enormous part of it that we still do not know) would never have come into being. Perhaps this is why Jesus is said to have said, "before Abraham was, I am."[2] In the biblical idiom, Abraham derives from the name Abram, the father of height. Height symbolizes a raised, i.e.

spiritual consciousness. This spiritual origin enables Abram to become Abraham, the father of a multitude, which is the Hebrew meaning of his new name.[3] Again, in the biblical idiom, multitude or nation invariably symbolize an abundance of thoughts, or the effusion of a state of consciousness, which in turn can bring the spiritual ideas into the manifested reality. Jesus' statement simultaneously postulates the indestructibility of consciousness and the fact that consciousness, in some mode of being, precedes any and all physical manifestations. Jesus might as well have said: Before *the world was, I AM*.

It is abundantly clear that we, you and I, have inherited this seemingly enigmatic and individualized consciousness, which is the prerequisite for bringing virtual potential into the manifested reality. Thus from the Ineffable flows individualized consciousness which, in turn, is the means for "bringing out" new reality, or the ever changing new worlds we all live in. John the Divine, in his Revelation, expresses this concept thus: "There will be a new heaven and a new earth," and later "Behold, I make all things new."[4]

This is what I mean by the mode of Becoming.

In like fashion, as our individualized consciousness finds its expression through our physical bodies, we inherit at the sensual level (become aware of) a 'world' created by our own and other individualization's (souls). This is the end product of the purpose of our presence in the manifested universe: which is to convert the virtual into the subjective and then the subjective into the objective reality. When we do so in full awareness, we are said to create 'miracles'.

It is only in the here-and-now that we can participate in this creative process. In the esoteric 'heaven' there is only stasis. In other words, the state of consciousness which is in 'heaven' is the state of consciousness of absolute Stillness. While the Stillness is synonymous with absolute Bliss, It is in Its non-creative mode. As I keep repeating, we must never forget that God has no being other than in a mode of being.

Thus we can experience heaven at different levels.

At the physical level, heaven is best reflected by various religions, which offer their faithful a promise of 'physical' bliss to simulate the state of relative happiness. This sort of heaven is best portrayed by the religion of Islam. Here (at the level of fundamentalist interpretation) we have heaven compared to "rivers of water unstaling, rivers of milk unchanging in flavour, and rivers of wine—delight to the drinkers, river, too, of honey purified..."[5] Evidently this heaven is meant to represent a state of physical or sensual pleasure, particularly to one living in an arid environment. It would be quite meaningless to an Inuit living in the Canadian North. Such a heaven is limited to the, so-called, astral projection, or a heaven defined by our powers of imagination.

At the mental level we enter the field of mathematics, physics, scientific theory. We, as I have mentioned, visualize a pre-creation condition that harbors Infinite Potential of creative possibilities. This 'virtual' heaven has been repeatedly rediscovered by the more advanced proposals dealing with the Chaos theory. Ancient Greeks have assigned the word chaos to the state or condition of the world before its creation.[6] The Webster dictionary offers this definition of the word chaos: *confusion or confused mass of matter and infinite space supposed to have existed before the ordered universe*. How very similar to our present idea of "Virtual Heaven". The most fascinating aspect of the Chaos Theory is that apparently the *confused mass* is *not* as confused as we, or perhaps the Greeks before us, thought. The Babylonian confusion appears to have a predisposition to order, a tendency to become manifest in an orderly fashion, or as Charles Darwin would say, perhaps, towards natural selection, towards a greater order, greater good. To me, such a tendency also predisposes Chaos to harbor an inherent Intelligence. If we capitalize this word, we can assign it divine intervention in the creative process.

Another way to think of this process is to observe that the virtual particles can extend their existence by the action of an observer. In other words, the observer is the creator of the manifested universe. And the observer is you and I, or more accurately, your and my state of consciousness.

For those interested, there is much more about this in the concepts unveiled by the Quantum Theory.

Finally we advance to the mystical heaven.

This heaven is beyond sensual, emotional, or mental fathoming. The residence of God cannot be appreciated with either our senses or intellect. The best we can do, is to center our consciousness on what we intuitively suspect "must be" the attributes of the Source of All. The one thing we can safely assume is that neither time nor space, nor the Einsteinian spacetime can have anything to do with the 'highest' heaven. As mentioned before, it is that which is in a state of Eternal Silence, of ultimate Bliss. Someone once said that to describe heaven in terms of mathematics is impossible, but, perhaps, a wondrous melody might give us an idea what it might be like. The man who suggested this course is Leon Lederman, a Nobel laureate, not in philosophy or theology, but in experimental physics. It is that Reality from which the Single Consciousness emanates, individualizes Itself, shines Light upon Itself, and proceeds into a mode of becoming. It is the source of all that is, of Life, and, most of all from our point of view, of Love. It is this last attribute which enables us to find our way back to our Source, to climb back into the primordial, indeed eternal, womb of Being, perhaps so as to emerge once again, partake in a new, fresh process of Eternal Becoming.

And so on.
Worlds without end, Consciousness without beginning.
You and I.
Individualizations of a single Source.
Of God.

***

010212

FOOTNOTES

(1). That's 1/1,000,000,000,000,000,000,000 of one second.
(2). John 8:58.
(3). Refer to Kapuscinski, Stanislaw DICTIONARY OF BIBLICAL SYMBOLISM [Inhousepress, Montreal 2001. Also available as eBook]
(4). Revelation 21: 1 and 5.
(5). Arberry, R.J. (translation), THE KORAN, Interpreted, [Simon and Shuster, New York 1996] VOL. II, XLVII *Muhammad*, p. 221.
(6). Originally the Greek: *chaos* meant empty space, abyss.

A good tree cannot bring forth evil fruit.

Matthew 7:18

A Word about the Author

Stanislaw Kapuscinski, (aka **Stan I.S. Law**), architect, sculptor and prolific writer was educated in Poland and England. Since 1965 he has resided in Canada. His special interests cover a broad spectrum of arts, sciences and philosophy. His fiction and non-fiction attest to his particular passion for the scope and the development of Human Potential. He authored more than thirty books, twenty of them novels.

Under his real name he published seven non-fiction books sharing his vision of reality. He also composed two collections of poems in his original native tongue in which he satirizes his view of the world while paying homage to Bozena Happach's sculptures.

Finally, he and his wife publish two blogs online, which, to date of this printing have been already visited by hundreds of thousands of people. We both hope you'll enjoy them as much.

Acknowledgments

I would be remiss were I not to thank my many friends for their comments, advice, and proofreading, none more so than Madeleine Witthoeft who's editing raised this book to acceptable literary standards. As always my gratitude to my wife, Bozena Happach, who put up with being a grass widow for weeks on end, and then offered me her inspired insights.

Sincerely,
Stanisław Kapuściński

Smashwords wrote in their Annual Review:

If you write a book that touches your readers' soul, or inspires them with passion or knowledge, your readers will market your book for you.

I've done my part. The rest is up to you.
And if you enjoyed my efforts, please write a (brief) review. Your thoughts are important to me.

(The covers are, of course, in full colour)

INHOUSEPRESS, MONTREAL, CANADA
email: info@inhousepress.ca

www.ingramcontent.com/pod-product-compliance
Lightning Source LLC
Chambersburg PA
CBHW022355040426
42450CB00005B/188